QuickBooks® Pro 2011:
LEVEL 1 of 2

TRISHA (HAKOLA) CONLON
Chemeketa Community College

LABYRINTH
LEARNING™

El Sobrante, CA

QuickBooks Pro 2011: Level 1
by Trisha (Hakola) Conlon

Copyright © 2011 by Labyrinth Learning

Labyrinth Learning
P.O. Box 20818
El Sobrante, California 24820
800.522.9746
On the web at lablearning.com

President:
Brian Favro

Product Development Manager:
Jason Favro

Managing Editor:
Laura Popelka

Production Manager:
Rad Proctor

eLearning Production Manager:
Arl S. Nadel

Editorial/Production Team:
Donna Bacidore, Everett Cowan,
Sandy Jones

Indexing: Joanne Sprott

Interior Design:
Mark Ong, Side-by-Side Studios

Cover Design:
Words At Work

ITEM: 1-59136-377-2
ISBN-13: 978-1-59136-377-4

Manufactured in the United States of America.

10 9 8 7 6 5 4 3

Table of Contents

LESSON 5: BANKING WITH QUICKBOOKS   154

APPENDIX A: NEED TO KNOW ACCOUNTING   196

Quick Reference Tables

Preface

QuickBooks® Pro 2011: Level 1 provides essential coverage of QuickBooks 2011 software. Topics covered include an introduction to QuickBooks, basic accounting principles, backing up files, creating companies, working with vendors, working with customers, banking with Quick-Books, and more. By the end of this course, students will be well prepared for the challenges presented in *QuickBooks Pro 2011: Level 2.*

For almost two decades, Labyrinth Learning has been publishing easy-to-use textbooks that empower educators to teach complex subjects quickly and effectively, while enabling students to gain confidence, develop practical skills, and compete in a demanding job market. We add comprehensive support materials, assessment and learning management tools, and eLearning components to create true learning solutions for a wide variety of instructor-led, self-paced, and online courses.

Our textbooks follow the *Labyrinth Instruction Design,* our unique and proven approach that makes learning easy and effective for every learner. Our books begin with fundamental concepts and build through a systematic progression of exercises. Quick Reference Tables, precise callouts on screen captures, carefully selected illustrations, and minimal distraction combine to create a learning solution that is highly efficient and effective for both students and instructors.

This course is supported with *comprehensive instructor support* materials that include printable solution guides for side-by-side comparisons, test banks, customizable assessments, customizable PowerPoint presentations, detailed lesson plans, pre-formatted files for integration to leading learning management system, and more. Our unique WebSims allow students to perform realistic exercises for tasks that cannot be performed in the computer lab.

Our *eLab assessment and learning management tool* is available to supplement this course. eLab is an intuitive, affordable, web-based learning system that helps educators spend less time on course management and more time teaching. eLab integrates seamlessly with your Labyrinth textbook.

Visual Conventions

This book uses many visual and typographic cues to guide students through the lessons. This page provides examples and describes the function of each cue.

`Type this text`	Anything you should type at the keyboard is printed in this typeface.
	Tips, Notes, and Warnings are used throughout the text to draw attention to certain topics.
Command→ Command→ Command, etc.	This convention indicates how to give a command from the Ribbon. The commands are written: Ribbon Tab→Command Group→Command→ Subcommand.
FROM THE KEYBOARD Ctrl + S to save	These margin notes indicate shortcut keys for executing a task described in the text.

Exercise Progression

The exercises in this book build in complexity as students work through a lesson toward mastery of the skills taught.

- **Develop Your Skills** exercises are introduced immediately after concept discussions. They provide detailed, step-by-step tutorials.
- **Reinforce Your Skills** exercises provide additional hands-on practice with moderate assistance.
- **Apply Your Skills** exercises test students' skills by describing the correct results without providing specific instructions on how to achieve them.
- **Critical Thinking** exercises are the most challenging. They provide generic instructions, allowing students to use their skills and creativity to achieve the results they envision.

Acknowledgements

We are grateful to the instructors who have used Labyrinth titles and suggested improvements to us over the many years we have been writing and publishing books. This book has benefited greatly from the reviews and suggestions of the following instructors.

Joanna Acri, *Cumberland Perry AVTS*

Kris Ball, *Dodge City Community College*

Elaine Barnwell, *Bevill State Community College*

Cindy Baucom, *Stanly Community College*

Dave Beetham, *Whatcom Community College*

Errol Belt, *San Juan Unified School District, Sunrise Tech Center*

Skochii Bennett-Polchlopek, *Quaboag Valley Community Development Corporation*

Marcia Bercot, *SkillSource*

Dwayne Briscoe, *Brazosport College*

Jim Britton, *River Valley Community College*

Paula Brown, *Durham Tech Community College*

Milt Cohen, *LAUSD - DACE*

Joan Cook, *Milwaukee Area Technical College*

Robert Cook, *Martinez Adult Education*

Patricia Cort, *Pat Cort's Word Procesing & Computer Training*

Pamela Doyle, *River Valley Community College*

Michael Ford, *The Ford Group*

Michael Fox, *Eastern Arizona College*

Candy Goff, *EHOVE Adult Career Center*

Stephanie Henderson, *Wildes & Company, PLLC*

Sonya Hendrix, *Central Technology Center*

Lyle Hicks, *Danville Area Community College*

Lisa Hull, *University of Phoenix and Boone County Learning Network*

Trixie Ingram, *Rich Mountain Community College*

Carol Jensen, *Cabrillo College*

Margaret Jones, *William Rainey Harper College*

Shawn Kendall, *Knox County Career Center*

Stacy Kildal, *Kildal Services LLC*

Joan Kistler, *Monroe Career and Technical Institute*

Marsha Kitter, *Brunswick Community College*

Sherry Leneve, *Montana State University*

Mary Lisovitch, *Youngstown State Metro College*

Sue Lobner, *Nicolet Area Technical College and Anderson Metz LTD*

Teresa Loftis, *San Bernardino Adult School*

Michelle L. Long, *Johnson County Community College*

Kay McGrath, *Foothill Adult Center – Grossmont Union High School District*

Cynthia McGuckin, *Trident Technical College*

Cheryl McKay, *Monroe County Community College*

Becky Newman, *Dixie Applied Technology College*

Susan Noble, *MiraCosta College*

Monika Olsen, *Liberty Adult Education*

Kris Perry, *Terra State Community College*

Lucretia Piercy, *A-B Technical College*

Mary Ann Powell, *SUNY Adirondack, WSWHE BOCES, Columbia-Greene Community College*

Carla Ralston, *Bookkeeping Plus*

Karolina Rasa, *CUNY Kingsborough Community College*

Winston Richard, *SOWELA Technical Community College*

Doris Scott, *Traviss Career Center*

Tabitha Smith, *Franklin Technology*

Tami Stewart, *Newberry County Career Center*

Carla Suehowicz, *Columbia College*

Carl Swoboda, *Southwest Tennessee Community College*

Sue Timothy, *Uintah Basin Applied Technology College*

Jim Turnbough, *Downey Adult School*

Cyndi Vandenbark, *Northeastern Junior College*

Mary Wildman, *Seneca Valley School District*

Michele Wilkens, *Minnesota State Community and Technical College Detroit Lakes Campus*

Daniel Wirkus, *Riverland Community College*

1

Introducing QuickBooks Pro

LESSON OBJECTIVES

After studying this lesson, you will be able to:

- Discuss basic accounting concepts
- Determine if QuickBooks is right for your business
- Manage basic QuickBooks files
- Open a portable company file
- Work with the QuickBooks window
- Back up a company file

QuickBooks has become the software of choice for many owners of small- and medium-sized businesses. No doubt, this is due to the multitude of functions and features that the software offers the smaller company. In this lesson, you will explore the various editions of QuickBooks and determine which is right for you. You will also examine what goes on behind the scenes and why it is so important for you to have a basic understanding of accounting. Finally, you will be introduced to some QuickBooks basics that are vital to your success as a QuickBooks user.

1.1 Discovering What's New in QuickBooks 2011

Each year, Intuit introduces a new version of QuickBooks with either new or improved features. As you work through this book, you will see these new aspects of the software called to your attention with a special icon.

 This is how you will be able to identify new or improved QuickBooks features.

Following is a list of some of the new features found in QuickBooks 2011.

- The Collections Center is a new tool that will help you to easily identify customers who have overdue balances, and it provides contact information at your fingertips. You will have a chance to work with this tool in *QuickBooks Pro 2011: Level 2*.

- Many businesses may encounter the situation where they create invoices that are basically the same for a number of customers. The new batch invoicing feature that will be covered in *QuickBooks Pro 2011: Level 2* will help you learn how to efficiently deal with this situation.

- The Customer Snapshot has been improved and will be explored in *QuickBooks Pro 2011: Level 2*.

- Just in Time transaction history for customers and vendors allows you to see summary information when entering a transaction for a customer or vendor. This time-saving feature will be covered in Lesson 4, Working with Customers.

- Online Backup has been enhanced for QuickBooks 2011 and will be discussed in this lesson.

- Printing to PDF files has been improved and made more reliable in QuickBooks 2011. You will learn more about it in Lesson 5, Banking with QuickBooks.

- QuickBooks users will now be able to use their web-based email accounts (the largest ones are supported) to email information from QuickBooks. You will have a chance to see how this works in *QuickBooks Pro 2011: Level 2*.

- A new Search feature is available that improves upon the Find feature. It allows you to search through all areas of QuickBooks to find text and coverage. You will learn about this in *QuickBooks Pro 2011: Level 2*.

- There are two additional snapshots available for your use: Customer and Payments. You will have an opportunity to learn more about these in Lesson 5, Banking with QuickBooks.

1.2 Presenting QuickBooks Pro

QuickBooks is a software program that allows companies to:

- Keep track of customers, vendors, employees, and other important entities
- Process sales transactions and cash receipts
- Process purchase transactions and payments to vendors
- Run payroll
- Track and sell inventory
- Run end-of-period financial reports
- Track assets (what you own) and liabilities (what you owe)
- Keep track of bank accounts
- Collaborate with accountants easily and efficiently

Types of Companies That Use QuickBooks Pro

QuickBooks Pro works well for different types of companies in a variety of industries. Ideally, your company should not have more than twenty employees and $1 million in annual revenue if you plan to use QuickBooks Pro (these are not strict rules, but guidelines). If your company is larger, you may want to consider using QuickBooks Enterprise Solutions. One type of business that QuickBooks Pro is not suited for is manufacturing, but Intuit has produced both Premier and Enterprise editions of QuickBooks especially for the manufacturing industry.

Aside from these issues, QuickBooks Pro can be customized and works well for many businesses, including not-for-profit organizations.

Editions of QuickBooks

Before you purchase your copy of QuickBooks, you should evaluate what you need QuickBooks to do for you. There are several editions of QuickBooks, all of which perform the basic tasks required for small-business bookkeeping. This book requires at the minimum the use of QuickBooks Pro, but it can be used with the Premiere edition as well. If you are using a different edition, your screen may look a little bit different from what is displayed throughout this book.

Versions, as Compared to Editions

Now, don't let yourself become confused by the difference between editions and versions of QuickBooks. Intuit creates a new version of QuickBooks each year (such as QuickBooks 2009, 2010, or 2011). Each new version provides additional features that are new for that year. This book is designed for QuickBooks 2011, but once you learn how to use the features QuickBooks offers, it will be easy to switch between versions.

With each version, Intuit creates a multitude of editions from which a company may choose (such as QuickBooks Simple Start, QuickBooks Pro, QuickBooks Premier, and QuickBooks Enterprise Solutions). There is also an online edition of QuickBooks available that, for a monthly fee, allows you to access your company QuickBooks files via the Internet. Take a look at the student resource center for this book (labyrinthelab.com/qb11_level01) to determine which edition will work best for your company.

The Online Edition of QuickBooks

Many companies are now using the online editions (Basic and Plus) of QuickBooks. The online versions look very similar to the traditional desktop editions but have some unique features, such as:

- The ability to access QuickBooks from any computer with Internet access, as well as from many popular smart phones
- A way for users in multiple or remote locations to utilize a single file
- Automatic online backups

In addition, there is no need to worry about technological problems associated with desktop product installation and support when using QuickBooks online.

All of the users of a company file can access it through the web with a username and password, and all users work with the same up-to-date company file. It is recommended that you have a high-speed Internet connection to utilize this edition. The online edition, as with the desktop editions, allows you to set up users and determine the access level for each one.

The online interface is very similar to that of QuickBooks Pro, so once you learn the basics of the program from studying this book, you will be able to transfer your knowledge to the online edition. It is similar to learning to drive a Ford and then driving a Toyota—you will just need to familiarize yourself with the differences before you take off! You also have the ability to import your company data from a desktop edition of QuickBooks into your online account. You do not purchase software for the online edition but, instead, pay a monthly fee. Not all features are available in the online edition, though, so it is best to compare the different editions on the Intuit website in order to determine which is best suited for your company's needs. You can find a link to the online edition comparison as well as current pricing in the student resource center for this book (labyrinthelab.com/qb11_level01).

QuickBooks Add-Ins

There are many add-ins created by Intuit and additional third parties that can make your life easier when using QuickBooks. There are products out there that can assist with tasks such as order entry, customer management, credit card processing, collections, payroll, check printing, and many more! You can also find add-ins that have been developed for specific industries such as construction, retail, and farming, to name a few. If you wish to explore add-ins that may be helpful to you, check out the Intuit website or use an Internet search engine to search for third-party options.

Types of Tasks

There are many types of tasks you can perform with QuickBooks. The tasks can be broken down into two main categories: those that affect the accounting behind the scenes (activities and company setup) and those that do not (lists and reporting). The following table lists the four basic types of tasks covered in this book.

Task	Function
List (Database)	A list allows you to store information about customers, vendors, employees, and other data important to your business.
Activities	This feature affects what is happening behind the scenes. Activities can be easily entered on forms such as invoices or bills.
Company Setup	This feature takes you through the steps necessary to set up a new company in QuickBooks.
Reports	QuickBooks provides many preset reports and graphs that are easily customizable to meet your needs.

1.3 Understanding Basic Accounting

Many business owners use QuickBooks to keep their own books and attempt to just learn the software. QuickBooks is quite intuitive, but you will find yourself running into problems if you don't understand the accounting basics on which QuickBooks is based. If you want to make sure you have a more solid understanding of accounting, you may wish to consider the book, *The ABCs of Accounting*, also published by Labyrinth Learning.

An Accountant's Worst Nightmare (or Greatest Dream?)

Picture yourself as an accountant who has just received a QuickBooks file from a client. The client has no idea how accounting works and, to him, debit and credit are just types of plastic cards he carries in his wallet. In his file you find duplicate accounts in the Chart of Accounts, accounts created as the wrong type, items posted to incorrect accounts, accounts payable inaccuracies, and payroll inaccuracies (to name just a few problems).

Now, as an accountant, you can consider this a nightmare because you will have to run numerous diagnostics to find all the mistakes (which could have been easily avoided if your client learned how to use QuickBooks properly in the first place) or a dream because your billable hours will increase at a rapid rate.

This scenario is exactly the reason why you, as the client, need to learn what happens behind the scenes in QuickBooks, as well as how to use the day-to-day functions of the software. By having a better understanding of the accounting and how to do things properly in the program, you will reduce the number of hours your accountant will have to spend and, thereby, save yourself the accountant fees in the end!

What's Up with GAAP?

GAAP stands for *generally accepted accounting principles*. These are accounting rules used to prepare, present, and report financial statements for a wide variety of entities. The organization that creates the rules is called the FASB (Financial Accounting Standards Board). Publicly owned companies need to follow these rules unless they can show that doing so would produce information that is misleading. It is wise for the small-business owner to adhere to GAAP. These rules work to make taxation fair as it affects small-business owners.

As GAAP attempt to achieve basic objectives, it has several basic assumptions, principles, and constraints. Throughout the book you will see reminders of how GAAP apply to tasks that you are completing in QuickBooks via the "Flashback to the GAAP" feature.

QUICK REFERENCE	OUTLINING GENERALLY ACCEPTED ACCOUNTING PRINCIPLES (GAAP)
Principle	**Description**
Business entity principle	The first assumption of GAAP is that the business is separate from the owners and from other businesses. Revenues and expenses of the business should be kept separate from the personal expenses of the business owner.
The assumption of the going concern	This principle assumes that the business will be in operation indefinitely.
Monetary unit principle	This principle assumes that a stable currency is going to be the unit of record.
Time-period principle	This principle implies that the activities of the business can be divided into time periods.
Cost principle	When a company purchases assets, it should record them at cost, not fair market value. For example, if you bought an item worth $750 for $100, it should be recorded at $100.
Revenue principle	This principle requires publicly traded companies (not always sole proprietorships) to record when the revenue is realized and earned, not when cash is received (accrual basis of accounting).
Matching principle	Expenses need to be matched with revenues. If a contractor buys a specific sink for a specific bathroom, it is matched to the cost of remodeling the bathroom. If there is no connection, then the cost may be charged as an expense to the project. This principle allows a better evaluation of the profitability and performance (how much did you spend to earn the revenue?).
Objectivity principle	This principle outlines that the statements of a company should be based on objectivity.
Materiality principle	When an item is reported, its significance should be considered. An item is considered significant when it would affect the decision made regarding its use.
Consistency principle	This principle means that the company uses the same accounting principles and methods from year to year.
Prudence principle	This principle means that if one needs to choose between two solutions, the one that will be least likely to overstate assets and income should be selected.

INTRODUCING "BEHIND THE SCENES"
Throughout this book you will see a special section called "Behind the Scenes" whenever you are learning about an activity performed within QuickBooks. This section will go over the accounting that QuickBooks performs for you when you record a transaction. Please note that the account names used in this feature use QuickBooks, rather than traditional accounting, nomenclature.

Accrual vs. Cash Basis Accounting

There are two ways that companies can choose to keep the books. The method you choose to implement depends on the nature of your business. QuickBooks makes it easy for you to produce reports utilizing either method, and your data entry will be the same regardless of which method you choose. Talk to your accountant or tax advisor to determine which method you have been using (for an existing business) or should use (for a new business).

Accrual Basis

In the accrual basis of accounting, income is recorded when the sale is made and expenses recorded when accrued. This method is often used by firms and businesses with large inventories. As you just learned from the GAAP table, this is the basis you need to use for publicly traded corporations.

Cash Basis

In the cash basis of accounting, income is recorded when cash is received and expenses recorded when cash is paid. This method is commonly used by small businesses and professionals involved in occupations that are not publicly traded.

> **FLASHBACK TO GAAP: REVENUE**
>
> Remember that publicly traded companies are able to record when the revenue is realized and earned—not when cash is received (accrual basis of accounting).

Where to Find More Help

You can learn more about accounting fundamentals in Appendix A, Need to Know Accounting, at the back of this book. It provides some basic definitions, theories, and a link to a web page with online resources. More in-depth coverage of accounting concepts can be found in the Labyrinth Learning book, *The ABCs of Accounting*.

In Appendix A, Need to Know Accounting, you will find information on:

- The accounting equation
- Debits and credits
- Types of accounts and normal balances

Introducing the Integrative Case Studies

In this book, you will follow the operations of a company called Chez Devereaux Salon and Spa for the Develop Your Skills exercises. This company provides hair care and spa services to clients. In *QuickBooks Pro 2011: Level 2*, you will be working with Rock Castle Construction, a construction company that deals with both service and inventory items.

In addition to the Develop Your Skill exercises, you will also have an opportunity to further hone your QuickBooks skills with Reinforce Your Skills exercises that deal with the Tea Shoppe at the Lake, a café and small retail store, and with Apply Your Skills exercises that allow you to work with Wet Noses Veterinary Clinic. The Develop Your Skill exercises will focus on using the Home page to perform tasks, while the Reinforce Your Skills exercises will primarily use the menu bar since that is a preference for some QuickBooks users. Once you are on your own with QuickBooks, you should use whichever method(s) you prefer.

The exercises that you will complete for Chez Devereaux, the Tea Shoppe at the Lake, and Wet Noses are set in the time frame of May through July 2011. Rock Castle Construction will be set in the time frame of December 2014 through January 2015. Each exercise step that includes a date will have you set the correct date within these time frames.

At the end of each lesson there are also Critical Thinking exercises that will challenge you further. There will be a "Sort Through the Stack" Critical Thinking exercise in each lesson that will sit you down at the desk of a woman who runs a not-for-profit organization. You will "look through" all of the papers at her desk and make the necessary entries into QuickBooks. In addition, you will be able to hone your skills using the main company file from the lesson in the Tackle the Tasks Critical Thinking exercises.

1.4 Managing Basic QuickBooks Files

Before you can begin working with a QuickBooks file, you need to understand some basic file management operations. This section will cover how to launch the program, store files, and restore QuickBooks portable company files.

Launching the Program

There is more than one way to do just about everything on a computer, and launching Quick-Books is no exception. Each computer is set up a little differently and may have different options for launching the program depending on shortcuts that have been created. Ask your instructor how he wishes for you to launch QuickBooks in your computer lab. Depending on the version of Windows you are running, QuickBooks will be found in the All Programs or Programs menu accessed via the Start button. Or there may be a shortcut to QuickBooks on the Windows Desktop.

 "There is more than one way to do just about everything on a computer" is not meant to confuse you! You will be introduced to various ways to perform tasks in QuickBooks. Choose whichever methods work best for you and stick with them.

Types of QuickBooks Files

There are three different types of files in which you can store your QuickBooks data: company files, backup files, and portable company files. The type of file that you will utilize when working with your business is the company file. A backup file is used to store a copy of your file in case your main file becomes corrupted and needs to be restored. A portable company file is much smaller than both company and backup files and is a convenient way to send your company information by email.

There are two other QuickBooks file types that play important support roles for your company data. A network data file has a file extension of .nd, and it contains important configuration data. A transaction log has a file extension of .tlg, and it can help you to recover any data entered after the last backup operation you have performed.

Your company file can be stored anywhere on your computer. The QuickBooks default storage location is the QuickBooks folder for the current version you are using.

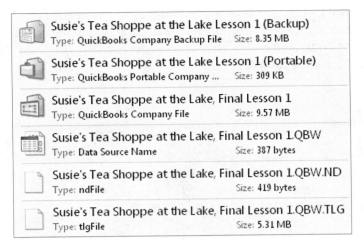

When QuickBooks creates either a backup or a portable company file, it compresses all data stored in the company file. This is why these files are substantially smaller than the company file. Notice how much smaller the portable company file is than the backup file. This is why portable company files are great for sending by email. The other types of files are "auxiliary" files in that they do not store your company data but play important support roles for the other file types.

Even though .nd and .tlg. files do not allow you to work with your company information, do *not* delete them. This can affect the integrity of your company data.

Opening and Restoring QuickBooks Files

In order to open a QuickBooks company file, or to restore either a backup or portable company file, you access the command via the File menu. QuickBooks doesn't save files as other programs like word-processing programs do. When you enter transactions, they are saved automatically to the QuickBooks file. To save a QuickBooks file for backup purposes, you create a compressed file—either a backup or portable company file. The act of decompressing a backup or portable company file for use is called restoring.

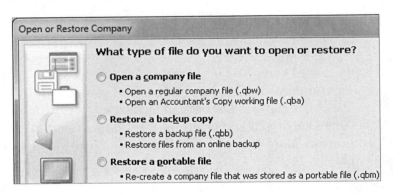

When you choose to open or restore a company from the file menu, you will see this window. It allows you to choose which type of file you will be accessing.

QUICK REFERENCE	OPENING AND RESTORING QUICKBOOKS DATA FILES
Task	**Procedure**
Open a QuickBooks company file	▪ Choose File→Open or Restore Company from the menu bar.
	▪ Choose Open a company file, and then click Next.
	▪ Navigate to the file you wish to open, select it, and then click Open.

QUICK REFERENCE	OPENING AND RESTORING QUICKBOOKS DATA FILES (continued)
Task	**Procedure**
Restore a backup file	■ Choose File→Open or Restore Company from the menu bar. ■ Choose Restore a backup copy, and then click Next. ■ Navigate to where the backup copy you wish to restore is located, either locally or online, and then click Next. ■ Locate the backup copy you wish to restore, and then click Open. ■ Click Next, choose the location to which you want the restored company file to be saved, and then click Save.
Restore a portable company file	■ Choose File→Open or Restore Company from the menu bar. ■ Choose Restore a portable file, and then click Next. ■ Navigate to the portable file you wish to restore, and then click Open. ■ Click Next, choose the location to which you want the restored company file to be saved, and then click Save. ■ Be patient, as it does take longer for portable company files to be restored than backup copies! Click OK to acknowledge the successful restoration.

DEVELOP YOUR SKILLS 1.4.1

Restore a Portable Company File

In this exercise, you will restore a QuickBooks portable company file.

Before You Begin: *Navigate to the student resource center for this book at labyrinthelab.com/qb11_level01 and view the "Downloading the Student Exercise Files" section of Storing Your Exercise Files. There you will find instructions on how to retrieve the student exercise files for this book and to copy them to your file storage location for use in this and future lessons.*

In the following step, you may see one of two editions of QuickBooks installed on your computer: Pro or Premier. This book works with both of these versions, so choose whichever version is installed.

1. Click the **Start** button, choose **All Programs**, choose **QuickBooks**, and choose **QuickBooks 2011**.

 A "splash screen" displays the version of QuickBooks you are launching and opens the program window.

2. Choose **File** from the menu bar, and then choose the **Open or Restore Company** command on the menu.

In the future, a menu bar command like this will be written as Choose File→Open or Restore Company from the menu bar.

 QuickBooks displays the Open or Restore Company window.

3. Click in the circle to the left of **Restore a portable file**.

4. Click **Next**.

5. Follow these steps to restore your file:

A Navigate to the file storage location you selected when you downloaded the student exercise files for this book.

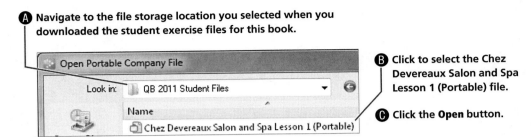

B Click to select the Chez Devereaux Salon and Spa Lesson 1 (Portable) file.

C Click the **Open** button.

6. Click **Next**, and then follow these steps to determine where the resulting company file will be located:

A Navigate to your file storage location.

B Replace Lisa's name with your own (e.g., the author's filename would be Trish's Chez Devereaux Salon and Spa).

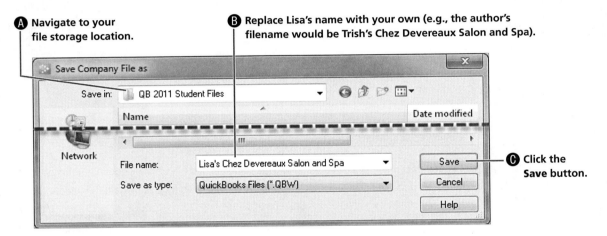

C Click the **Save** button.

It may take a few moments for the portable company file to open. The QuickBooks window opens with the Chez Devereaux Salon and Spa company file ready to go. Leave this window open for the next exercise.

7. Click **OK** to close the QuickBooks Information window.

8. Click **No** in the Set Up External Accountant User window, if necessary.

1.5 Working with the QuickBooks Window

There are many screen elements with which you are probably familiar if you have ever worked with a Windows-based PC. Many of the elements remain very similar regardless of the program in which you are operating. The elements in common are the title bar and quick-sizing buttons. In addition, many programs utilize menu and tool/icon bars that you can see in QuickBooks.

The title bar tells you the name of the company you are working with and the version/edition of QuickBooks you are using.

Click a button on the menu bar to see a drop-down menu of options specific to that button.

The icon bar displays icons that allow you to access common activities, centers, and lists with a single click of the mouse.

Notice the workflow diagram indicated by arrows on the Home page.

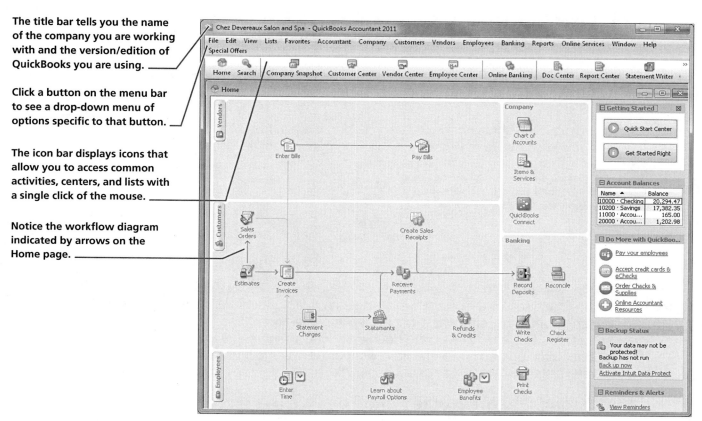

All commands accessible on the icon bar and Home page can be found through the menu bar, but the opposite is not true. (They would be a bit too crowded!)

Flowing Through the Home Page

The workflow diagram on the Home page is indicated by arrows going from one task icon to another. It is important to follow the diagram so as not to run into trouble. Some instances of trouble that you may encounter are listed below.

- If you write a check rather than pay a bill (for which a bill has been entered), you will overstate expenses.

- If you make a deposit rather than receive a payment for an invoiced amount, you will overstate income.

Sales tax errors can also occur by not following the proper flow outlined on the Home page.

QuickBooks Connect

With QuickBooks 2011, Intuit introduced QuickBooks Connect, which allows users to access their QuickBooks data online or on their mobile phones. (Not all phones are supported. To find out if your phone will work with this feature, visit the student resource center for a link to the most current information.) To access this service and learn more, click the task icon in the Company area of the Home page.

The QuickBooks Connect task icon can be found in the Company area of the Home page.

Controlling the QuickBooks Display

If you cannot see the icon bar or Open Windows list, you can turn them on through the View menu. To show or hide the icon bar, choose View→Icon Bar from the menu bar. To show or hide the Open Windows list, choose View→Open Window List from the menu bar.

You can switch between windows by clicking them in the Open Windows list, much the same as you switch between windows by clicking buttons on the Windows taskbar.

A checkmark next to Icon Bar on the View menu tells you that this element is currently displayed on the screen.

Note where you can go to customize the icon bar.

To single-click or double-click—that is the question. In QuickBooks you will single-click most of the time. Make it a rule to always single-click first; double-click only if the single-click doesn't work. Most students are "happy double-clickers," and this can get you into trouble sometimes (especially if you are double-clicking a toggle button, which would be like flipping a light switch up and down and then wondering why the light didn't stay on). Remember, you always single-click a button and a hyperlink!

Customizing the Home Page

QuickBooks allows users to customize the Home page based on their preferences and how they use the software. The task icons displayed on the Home page will change when a user makes changes to certain preferences. For instance, if a user decides to track inventory in QuickBooks and so turns on the "Inventory and purchase orders are active" preference, additional task icons will be added to the Vendor area of the Home page to assist with the inventory-related tasks. You will learn how to change this preference in *QuickBooks Pro 2011: Level 2*. Changes to other preferences that result in changes to the Home page will be dealt with throughout this book as well.

When you make a change to a preference that will change the content of the Home page, you will see this Warning window appear. QuickBooks has to close the open windows in order to make the change to the Home page.

In addition, you can choose to not display some of the task icons that you may not use as often. The commands will still be available through the menu, just not accessible via a task icon on the Home page.

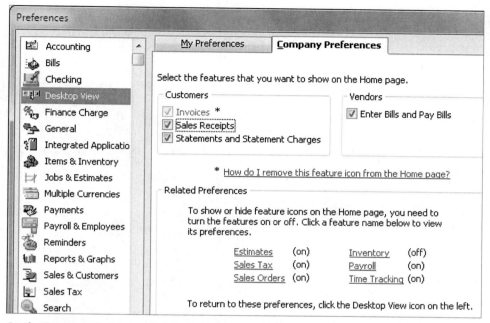

On the Company Preferences tab in the Desktop View category, you can choose to not display task icons for tasks that you may not use as often in order to "unclutter" your Home page. The task icons can be added back at any time by returning to the Preferences window and reselecting the option.

Exiting QuickBooks

When you are finished working with QuickBooks, you will need to close the company file and the program. This can be accomplished by clicking the Close button at the top-right corner of the QuickBooks window or by selecting File→Exit from the menu bar.

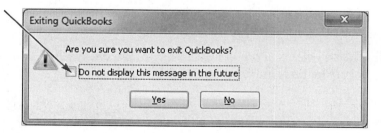

If you choose to exit QuickBooks by clicking the Close button at the top-right corner of the window, you will see a warning message that you are exiting QuickBooks. Notice that you can choose to not have this message appear again by clicking in the checkbox.

Close All Windows with One Command

If you have a lot of windows open and wish to close them all simultaneously, QuickBooks makes it easy with the Close All command. This command can be accessed by choosing Windows from the menu bar.

Task Icon ToolTips

There are many task icons on the Home page. As you customize your QuickBooks file, you may see more or fewer appear, depending on how you use the program. If you are not sure what a certain task item is used for, simply "mouse over" it (place your mouse pointer over the icon and hold it still, without clicking), and a ToolTip that explains what the task will accomplish for you will appear.

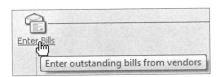

Notice that when you "mouse over" the Enter Bills task icon, a ToolTip appears to explain what task you can accomplish if you click the icon.

Live Community

When you open QuickBooks 2011, a "Have a Question?" window with the Live Community feature opens to the right of your main QuickBooks window by default. The Live Community is a place where you can collaborate with other QuickBooks users to get advice or to provide your own insights.

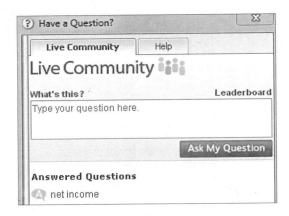

DEVELOP YOUR SKILLS 1.5.1

Explore the QuickBooks Window

In this exercise, you will have a chance to explore the QuickBooks window.

Explore the QuickBooks Window

1. Click the **Vendors** button on the Home page.
   The Vendor Center will open, from where you can work with the vendors on your list, manage various vendor transactions, and create new vendors.

2. Choose **Lists→Chart of Accounts** from the menu bar.
   The Chart of Accounts window opens. This is an example of a list in QuickBooks. It lists the various accounts this company utilizes.

3. Click the **Company Snapshot** icon on the icon bar.
   The Company Snapshot window opens.

4. Choose **View→Open Window List** from the menu bar.
   Notice that all four of the open windows are listed.

5. Click the **Chart of Accounts** item on the Open Window List.

The Chart of Accounts window appears on top of the other windows and becomes the active window. Look at the windows you have opened within QuickBooks and notice that each one has its own set of quick-sizing buttons (Close, Restore/Maximize, Minimize). You can use these buttons to control the display of each window within the QuickBooks program window.

6. Click the **Close** [×] button for the Chart of Accounts window.

7. Choose **Window→Close All** from the menu bar.
   This command will close all open windows for you so you don't have to go chasing "Xs" around the screen! Notice that the Home page is closed since it is a window, but that the Open Windows List is still displayed since it is not.

8. Close the Open Windows List by choosing **View→Open Window List** from the menu bar.

9. Choose **View→Icon Bar** from the menu bar.
   QuickBooks no longer displays the icon bar.

Exit and Reopen QuickBooks

10. Choose **File→Exit** from the menu bar.
    The QuickBooks window closes.

11. Open QuickBooks by choosing **Start→All Programs→QuickBooks→ QuickBooks 2011**.
    Notice that QuickBooks opens the file that you were last working on and that the icon bar is not visible. The Home page will be visible, though, as it is set to open whenever QuickBooks is launched. This is a preference that can be changed, if desired.

12. Click **No** in the Set Up an External Accountant User window, if necessary.

13. **Maximize** the QuickBooks program window, if necessary.

14. Choose **View→Icon Bar** from the menu bar.
    The icon bar reappears.

Mouse Around the Home Page

15. Mouse over the task icon for the following tasks on the Home page, and then write the ToolTips in the spaces provided. If you do not wish to write in the book, you can print a worksheet for this exercise from the book's website.

    ■ Chart of Accounts

    _____

    _____

    ■ Create Invoices

    _____

    _____

    ■ Pay Bills

    _____

    _____

    ■ Reconcile

    _____

    _____

Leave QuickBooks open with the Home page displayed for the next exercise.

1.6 Backing Up and Updating Your Company File

You have already learned how to restore a portable company file. Now you will learn how to create a backup file. If you have ever lost a file or had your computer "crash" on you, you can surely understand the importance of backing up your data!

When working in QuickBooks, you cannot save your file as you may be used to doing in programs such as Microsoft® Word. Transactions are automatically saved to your company file as you enter them, so the backup operation will back up the entire file.

How often you back up your file is up to you, but you should not let too much time go between backups. If you lose your company file and are forced to restore the backup copy, you will have to enter all of the transactions since your last backup.

Backup Location

Do not back up your company file to your hard drive or where your main company file is stored. Choose an alternate backup location such as a network drive, USB drive, CD-RW, or the QuickBooks' online backup option. If you back up your file to a USB drive or some other removable media, make sure to store the backup copy someplace other than where the original file is physically located. For instance, do not set the backup disc on the PC where the original file is, just in case something such as fire or water damage occurs at the physical location.

Online Backup Options

Online backup is now fully integrated in QuickBooks 2011.

In order to ensure the security of your QuickBooks data in the event of human error, natural disaster, or a computer crash, you may wish to back up your QuickBooks data online. Quick-Books offers an online backup option for a monthly fee that is determined based on the amount of room you wish to have available for your backup work. You can schedule your backups to happen automatically or manually with this service. When your files are uploaded, they are encrypted and sent to a remote location from where you can access them from any location via the Internet. You can find out more about this service by following the steps outlined in the next Quick Reference table.

When to Save a Backup Copy

In QuickBooks, you have the opportunity to choose when you wish to back up your company file. QuickBooks allows you to choose between three options:

- Immediately
- Immediately and schedule future backups
- Only schedule future backups

The future backup options make it easy to back up your company file on a regular basis without having to remember to physically issue the command. If you choose scheduled backups, make sure that your selected backup location is available to QuickBooks at the scheduled times. For instance, ensure that you have your USB flash drive available if that is your backup location.

Updating Your QuickBooks Company File

Earlier in this lesson you learned about the different versions of QuickBooks that are available for purchase each year. In addition, Intuit releases free updates for your QuickBooks software throughout the life of the version. (At some point, Intuit will announce that they will no longer support each version of QuickBooks based on the length of time since it was released.) These updates are available for download over the Internet and may include such things as a new service, a maintenance release, a new feature, or something else relevant to your company.

The easiest way to stay abreast of these updates is to have QuickBooks automatically check for and download them for you through the Automatic Update feature.

Verifying the QuickBooks Release Number

You can easily find out which release number you are working with for your current version of QuickBooks by tapping the [F2] key. This will launch a window that displays not just the release, but also a lot of other information about your QuickBooks file. In addition, if you choose to open the Update QuickBooks window from the Help menu, you can also find your release number displayed at the top of that window.

QUICK REFERENCE	BACKING UP AND UPDATING A QUICKBOOKS FILE
Task	**Procedure**
Create a portable company file	■ Choose File→Create Copy from the menu bar. ■ Choose Portable company file, and then click Next. ■ Choose the location in which to store the portable company file, and then click Save. ■ Click OK to allow QuickBooks to close and reopen your file. ■ Click OK to acknowledge the portable company file creation.
Create a backup file	■ Choose File→Create Backup from the menu bar. ■ Choose whether you wish to create a local or online backup, and then click Next. ■ Choose the location in which to store the backup copy, and then click OK. ■ Choose when you wish to create the backup copy, and then click Next. ■ Ensure the location for the backup file is correct, and then click Save. ■ Click OK to acknowledge the backup file creation.
Learn more about current online backup options	■ Choose File→Create Backup from the menu bar. ■ Click the Learn More link under the Online Backup option.
Set up QuickBooks to automatically update	■ Choose Help→Update QuickBooks from the menu bar. ■ Click the Options tab, and then choose Yes to Automatic Update your QuickBooks file. ■ Click Close.
Update QuickBooks manually	■ Choose Help→Update QuickBooks from the menu bar. ■ Click the Update Now tab, and then click to select/deselect the updates you wish to receive. ■ Click Get Updates.

Task	Procedure
Determine the release number of QuickBooks	■ Choose Help→Update QuickBooks from the menu bar. ■ With the Overview tab displayed, look at the top right of the Update QuickBooks window for the release number. *or* ■ Tap F2 to view all of the information in the Product Information window for your QuickBooks file, including the current release number.

Back Up Your QuickBooks Data File

In this exercise, you will create a backup copy of your company file. Ask your instructor where he wants you to back up your file. A USB removable storage drive is used in this example.

1. Choose **File→Create Backup** from the menu bar.

2. Click to choose **Local Backup**, and then click **Next**.

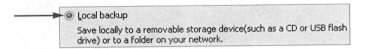

3. Click the **Browse** button.

4. Choose your file storage location in the **Browse for Folder** window. (The drive or folder name will probably be different from the one shown here.)

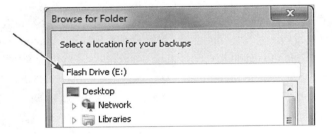

If you are not sure where to save your backup copy, ask your instructor or see Storing Your Exercise Files *in the student resource center for more information regarding file storage media.*

5. Click the **OK** button twice.
If you have chosen to save the file to the same drive on which the company file is stored, QuickBooks will display a warning window.

6. Read the information in the QuickBooks window, and then click the **Use this location** option, if necessary.

7. Choose **Save it now**, and then click **Next** again.

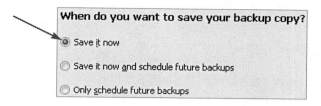

A Save Backup Copy window will appear and should display the file storage location you chose in step 4.

8. Ensure that the correct file storage location is displayed, and then click **Save**. *QuickBooks will first verify that your file is not corrupted and will then create a backup copy in the location you specified. A window will appear recommending that you use the Intuit Online Backup Service.*

9. Click **No, Thanks** to acknowledge the information window that shows where the backup file is located.

10. Choose the appropriate option for your situation:
    ▪ If you are continuing on to the next lesson or to the end-of-lesson exercises, leave QuickBooks open and move on to the next exercise.
    ▪ If you are finished working in QuickBooks for now, choose **File→Exit** from the menu bar.

1.7 Concepts Review

Concepts Review   labyrinthelab.com/qb11_level01

To check your knowledge of the key concepts introduced in this lesson, complete the Concepts Review quiz by going to the URL listed above.

Reinforce Your Skills

In all of the Reinforce Your Skills exercises, you will be working with a company called the Tea Shoppe at the Lake. This business sells food and drinks and provides catering services. Susie Elsasser is the proprietor of the business. You will assist Susie in a variety of QuickBooks tasks as you work your way through this book.

REINFORCE YOUR SKILLS 1.1
Find Your Way Around QuickBooks

In this exercise, you will take a look at Susie's QuickBooks company file. You will begin by opening a portable company file.

Restore a Portable Company File

1. Start **QuickBooks**, if necessary.

2. Choose **File→Open or Restore Company** from the menu bar.

3. Choose to **Restore** a portable file, and then click **Next**.

4. Follow these steps to select the file to restore:

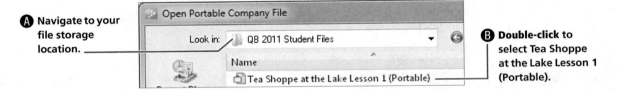

Ⓐ Navigate to your file storage location.

Ⓑ Double-click to select Tea Shoppe at the Lake Lesson 1 (Portable).

Double-clicking the filename works the same as if you had single-clicked the filename and then clicked the Open button.

5. Click **Next** to move to the next screen.

6. Follow these steps to choose where to locate your new company file:

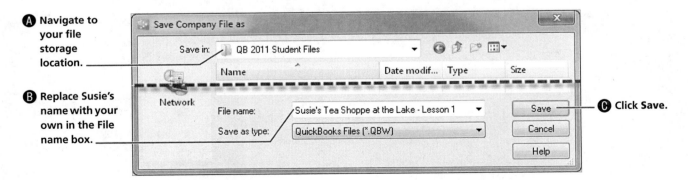

Ⓐ Navigate to your file storage location.

Ⓑ Replace Susie's name with your own in the File name box.

Ⓒ Click Save.

There is a long pause as QuickBooks opens the portable company file.

7. Click **OK** in the QuickBooks Information window.
   QuickBooks opens the company file and displays the Home page.

Navigate in the Company File

Now you will take some time to explore the QuickBooks window.

8. Open the Items List by clicking the **Items & Services** task icon in the Company area of the Home page.
QuickBooks displays the Item List window.

9. Open the **Customer Center** button on the icon bar.

10. Choose **Vendors→Enter Bills** from the menu bar.
QuickBooks displays an Enter Bills window, ready for you to enter a bill from a vendor.

11. Choose **View→Open Window List** from the menu bar.

12. Click the **Customer Center** item as shown to make it the active window.

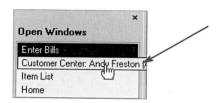

13. Choose **Window→Item List** from the menu bar.
This menu bar command produces the same result as clicking an open window on the Open Windows List. QuickBooks displays the selected window.

14. Choose **View→Open Window List** to close it.

15. Choose **Window→Close All** from the menu bar.
Notice that this command closes all open windows, including the Home page.

16. Click the **Home** icon on the icon bar.
QuickBooks displays the Home page.

17. Choose the appropriate option for your situation:
   - If you are continuing on to the next lesson or the rest of the end-of-lesson exercises, leave QuickBooks open.
   - If you are finished working in QuickBooks for now, choose **File→Exit** from the menu bar.

Practice Working with T-Accounts

In this exercise, you will use your accounting knowledge. You can write directly in the book or print a copy of the worksheet for this exercise from the student resource center. You may wish to refer to Appendix A for assistance, or if you have a copy of Labyrinth's The ABCs of Accounting, *that would be a helpful resource as well.*

Before You Begin: *(Optional) You can also print a copy of the worksheet from the student resource center for this book at labyrinthelab.com/qb11_level01.*

1. Using the following T accounts (or your printed worksheet), write the name of each of the accounts listed on the top of a T:
   - Bank Service Charges
   - Food Sales
   - Checking Account
   - Loan for Delivery Vehicle
   - Prepaid Insurance
   - Retained Earnings

2. Next to each account, write the type of account it is (asset, liability, equity, income, or expense).

3. Label the debit and credit side of each T.

4. Place an **NB** on the appropriate side of the T to indicate the normal balance of each account.

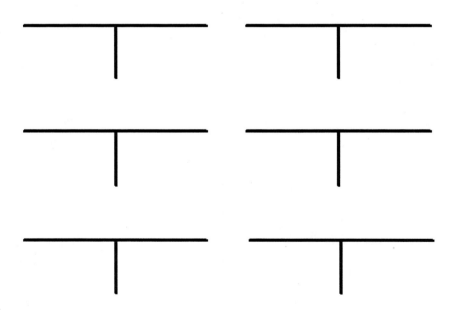

Apply Your Skills

In all of the Apply Your Skills exercises, you will be working with a company called Wet Noses Veterinary Clinic run by Dr. Sadie James, DVM. She is a small-animal vet specializing in dogs and cats.

APPLY YOUR SKILLS 1.1

Restore a QuickBooks Backup File

In this exercise, you will restore a backup file (up to this point you have been working with portable company files) and take a look at Dr. Sadie James' QuickBooks company file.

1. Start **QuickBooks** and restore the Wet Noses Veterinary Clinic-Lesson 1 portable company file. Make sure to name the restored company file **[Your first name]'s Wet Noses Veterinary Clinic.**

2. **Open** the following windows using any of the methods described in this lesson:
   - Create Invoice
   - Item List
   - Customer Center
   - Chart of Accounts
   - Pay Bills
   - Company Snapshot

3. Display the **Item List** window above the other open windows.

4. Ask your instructor to view your screen for this exercise.

5. Choose the appropriate option for your situation:
   - If you are continuing on to the next lesson, leave QuickBooks open.
   - If you are finished working in QuickBooks for now, choose **File→Exit** from the menu bar.

Get a Grasp on Accounting Principles

In this exercise, you will use your accounting knowledge to brainstorm the accounts that would be required for the business that you will be working with in the Apply Your Skills exercises throughout the rest of this book.

Before You Begin: *(Optional) You can also print a copy of the worksheet from the student resource center for this book at labyrinthelab.com/qb11_level01.*

1. Think about a veterinary practice. On the printed worksheet or in the following space, list the accounts that you feel would be required on the business's Chart of Accounts.

2. In the second column, list the type of account for each.

3. In the third column, state whether the normal balance for the account would be a debit or a credit.

Account Name	Account Type (Asset, Liability, Equity, Income, Expense)	Normal Balance (DR/CR)

Creating a Company

LESSON OBJECTIVES

After studying this lesson, you will be able to:

- Plan and create a company
- Edit your QuickBooks preferences and customize a company file
- Enter opening balances and historical transactions
- Run list reports and find help for QuickBooks
- Set up QuickBooks users
- Understand closing the books "QuickBooks style"

Now that you have had a chance to explore the QuickBooks window and learn about how to work with QuickBooks files, it is time to create a company file. By taking the knowledge that you gain from this lesson and coupling it with what you will learn in the rest of the book, you will be ready at the end of your QuickBooks studies to create a file for your own company.

Chez Devereaux Salon and Spa

Lisa Devereaux is a new small-business owner who has opened a small but upscale salon and spa in a serene wooded setting. She has three multi-licensed cosmetologists and one licensed massage therapist who will rent the space needed for creating quality services. There are three styling chairs for hair services and one private room available for massages and private waxing services.

Before creating this company, Lisa's friend Adrianna told her about QuickBooks and what it could do for her new company in terms of saving time and improving efficiency. Adrianna suggested that Lisa write down some important information in a checklist before starting her QuickBooks company.

Chez Devereaux Salon and Spa
Company Checklist for QuickBooks

Address:
444 North Pelham St.
Rhinelander, WI 54501

Fiscal year: January

Tax form: 1040

Accounting basis: Cash

Federal EIN: 99-9999999
State ID: 999-9999-9

Phone:
715.555.4010
715.555.4015 fax

Need from accountant: Chart of accounts, what should I use for items?

Vendors: need names, addresses, account numbers, and payment terms for each

Customers: need names and contact information, payment terms, and account numbering system

Start date: 4/30/2011

Lisa has written out the information she needs to have handy to start her new company file.

2.1 Planning and Creating a Company

Before you begin to set up your QuickBooks company, it is important to do some careful planning. You must think about the information you want to get from QuickBooks before you begin. As with many situations, garbage in will equal garbage out!

Choosing Your Start Date

Choosing the start date that is right for you is important. Very ambitious people may think they want to start their QuickBooks file the day they started their company. This is a nice idea, but not very practical for a busy or cost-conscious entrepreneur.

Keep in mind that you must enter all transactions for your company (invoices, checks, bills paid, etc.) from the start date forward. If you choose a date too far in the past, this process will take a long time to complete.

You should strive to start your QuickBooks company file at the beginning of a month, a quarter, or your fiscal year. You may want to discuss this matter with your accountant to help determine the best and most practical starting date for your business. The actual start date should be the last day of the prior period rather than the first day of the current period; for example, we will use 4/30/11 rather than 5/1/11.

The Five Ps

Sit down and think about what you want QuickBooks to do for you. It is difficult to go back and add a new field for every customer or change every transaction! A little planning at the beginning can save you a lot of time in the future. Think about the five Ps (Prior Planning Prevents Poor Performance) as you get ready to start your company and take into account the needs of all of the stakeholders involved. What type of information will each stakeholder need to be able to interact efficiently with your business? Potential stakeholders may include your accountant, customers, vendors, employees, stockholders, partners, etc.

How Many Companies Should You Create?

Generally, the best guideline is to set up a separate QuickBooks company file for each tax return you will file.

FLASHBACK TO GAAP: BUSINESS ENTITY

Remember that the business is separate from the owners and from other businesses. Revenues and expenses of the business should be kept separate from the personal expenses of the business owner. Also, revenue and expenses for separate companies must be kept separate from the other companies that may be operated by the same owner.

Creating a New QuickBooks File

There are several ways you can go about creating your new QuickBooks file. Look at the following list to determine which one will work best for your situation:

- Create a company from scratch
- Upgrade from a previous version of QuickBooks
- Convert from a different QuickBooks edition
- Convert a Quicken file
- Convert a Peachtree© file

Using an Old QuickBooks File as a Template for a New One

If you wish to create your new file based on an older one, QuickBooks will allow you to keep the lists and preferences from the old file while removing the old, unneeded transactions. Some QuickBooks users prefer to keep a separate company file for each fiscal year of the business, so being able to keep preferences and list data while removing transactions allows a person to easily do this.

To complete this task, you must clean up your company data from the old file using the Clean Up Company Wizard. Ensure you have a large window of time available before you start this process, as it can take some time to clean up a large file. QuickBooks will create a backup and archive copy of your file as a part of this process, as well as verify file integrity.

Choosing a Setup Path

When creating a new company from scratch, you must decide which path you want to take: EasyStep or Skip Interview.

When you choose to create a new company in QuickBooks, you will see this window, which allows you to choose the best method for you.

EasyStep

This method of company creation takes you through a series of questions. Your answer to each question determines how your company will be set up. The process is similar to wizards in Microsoft products or Intuit's Turbo Tax program. Keep in mind that this method takes much longer and requires more in-depth planning. You will have the opportunity to use this method in the Reinforce Your Skills section of this lesson.

Skip Interview

If you don't want to go through the lengthy interview process, you can choose to skip it. QuickBooks will ask you for basic information and then it will be up to you to set up certain items such as payroll and inventory later. You will use this method in the Develop Your Skills exercises in this lesson.

A Setup Checklist

There are some items that you should gather before you begin to set up your company. Review the checklist of items to collect in the student resource center for this book at labyrinthelab.com/qb11_level01.

A Quick Payroll Primer

You will be introduced to running payroll in QuickBooks in *QuickBooks Pro 2011: Level 2*. If you choose to create your new company using the Easy Step interview method, you need to understand a bit about how QuickBooks deals with payroll first.

If you wish to include an addition or deduction on an employee's paycheck, you must first set it up as a payroll item. During the EasyStep interview you will have an opportunity to create payroll items. If you will be using QuickBooks for payroll and wish to set it up during the setup process, you will need to have the following information ready.

- Information for each employee: name, address, social security number, and withholding information (from their W-4)
- All "additions" that will be found on a paycheck, such as salaries, hourly wages, and bonuses
- All payroll taxes the employees are required to pay
- All payroll taxes you, as the employer, are required to pay
- Any additional deductions you will be withholding from paychecks, such as investment plan contributions or child support payments

Your Starter Chart of Accounts

During the setup process, QuickBooks will ask you to choose the business type that your company most closely resembles. QuickBooks will use your choice to create a Chart of Accounts close to what you need. (It will take you less time to edit it to fit your unique business than to start from scratch.) QuickBooks will also create profile lists based on your selection. You will work with the customer and vendor profile lists in Lesson 3, Working with Vendors. Choose carefully here, as you cannot go back and change the business type option.

In order to ensure your books are set up properly, you should talk to your accountant to make sure that your chart of accounts is set up correctly. A quick conversation and small bill now can prevent a large bill in the future.

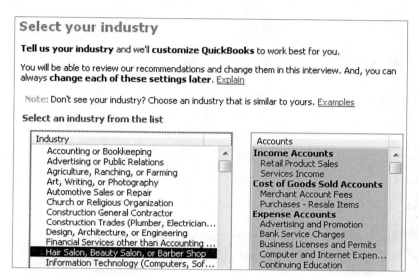

QuickBooks has several predefined company chart of accounts for specific industries that will help users in those or similar industries streamline their setup processes.

 Once you select a business type during the setup process, you cannot change it later. You can edit and delete accounts and list entries, though.

Account Beginning Balances

If you have an existing company for which you are setting up QuickBooks, you should enter the balances of all asset and liability accounts during the setup process (although you can enter them in the registers later). These account beginning balances are termed "opening balances" in QuickBooks. You will learn more about entering and editing these balances later in the lesson.

After you create your first balance sheet account, QuickBooks will create an Opening Balance Equity account, in which the account beginning balances you enter will be placed. Asset beginning balances credit the account, while liability beginning balances debit it. This account is created so you can have a balance sheet that is accurate even if you haven't entered all assets and liabilities for your company.

TYPES OF ACCOUNTS IN QUICKBOOKS

Account Type	Example	Normal Balance
Bank	Checking Account	Debit
Accounts Receivable	Accounts Receivable	Debit
Other Current Asset	Prepaid Rent	Debit
Fixed Asset	Machinery	Debit
Other Asset	Long Term Notes Receivable	Debit
Accounts Payable	Accounts Payable	Credit
Credit Card	Silver Falls Bank Visa	Credit
Other Current Liability	Short Term Loan	Credit
Long Term Liability	Auto Loan	Credit
Equity	Opening Balance Equity	Credit
Income	Sales	Credit
Cost of Goods Sold	Cost of Goods Sold	Debit
Expense	Telephone Expense	Debit
Other Income*	Interest Income	Credit
Other Expense*	Corporate Taxes	Debit

* Other Income and Other Expense accounts are used to track income and expenses that are not the result of normal day-to-day business operations.

QUICK REFERENCE — CREATING A NEW COMPANY FILE

Task	Procedure
Create a new company in QuickBooks	■ Go through the checklist to make sure you have all necessary information. ■ Plan what you want QuickBooks to do for you. ■ Choose File→New Company from the menu bar. ■ Choose the method you want to use to set up your company file in the EasyStep Interview window.
Edit information for a new company	■ Choose Company→Company Information from the menu bar. ■ Edit the information in the Company Information window.
Create a new company file based on a prior one, keeping list data and preferences	■ Choose File→Utilities→Clean Up Company Data from the menu bar. ■ Choose to either remove all transactions as of a specific date or all transactions in the file. ■ Continue through the wizard screens. ■ Click Begin Cleanup. ■ Click OK to close the message, and then click Create Back Up.

Create a New Company

In this exercise, you will skip the EasyStep interview and set up the company for Chez Devereaux Salon and Spa.

1. Launch **QuickBooks**.

2. Choose **File→New Company** from the menu bar.

3. Click the **Skip Interview** button.

4. Follow these steps to enter the company information:

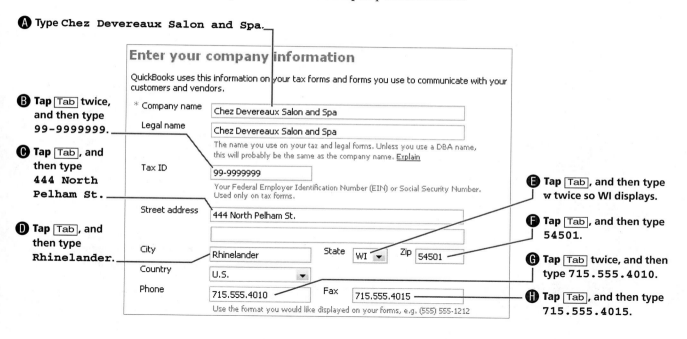

Ⓐ Type **Chez Devereaux Salon and Spa**.

Ⓑ **Tap** Tab **twice, and then type 99-9999999.**

Ⓒ **Tap** Tab **, and then type 444 North Pelham St.**

Ⓓ **Tap** Tab **, and then type Rhinelander.**

Ⓔ **Tap** Tab **, and then type w twice so WI displays.**

Ⓕ **Tap** Tab **, and then type 54501.**

Ⓖ **Tap** Tab **twice, and then type 715.555.4010.**

Ⓗ **Tap** Tab **, and then type 715.555.4015.**

You will need to type the phone numbers just as you wish them to appear on forms in this window—including punctuation such as parentheses, dashes, or periods. Be careful that you spell everything correctly when entering this company information. Imagine how embarrassing it would be to send out invoices, bills, and other correspondence with your own company name and information incorrect!

5. Click **Next** to continue with the new company setup.
   You can make future changes to this information by choosing Company→Company Information from the menu bar.

6. Click in the circle to choose **Sole Proprietorship** as the way in which your company is organized.

 If you choose Other/None at this stage, you will not be able to assign tax lines to your accounts. This means you will not be able to transfer your tax information to tax preparation software or run income tax reports.

7. Click **Next** twice, ensuring in the second screen that January is selected as the first month of your fiscal year.

8. Click to choose **Hair Salon, Beauty Salon, or Barber Shop** as the company type that most closely matches yours.

Take a moment to click the different company types on the left and view the resulting preset Chart of Accounts on the right.

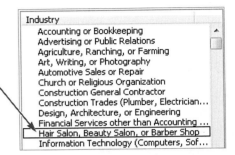

9. After exploring the different business types, make sure that Hair Salon, Beauty Salon, or Barber Shop is chosen, and then click **Next**.

10. Click **Next** once more.

QuickBooks will open a Filename for New Company window, in which you will set where the new company file will be located as well as the name for that new file.

11. Follow these steps to save your new QuickBooks file:

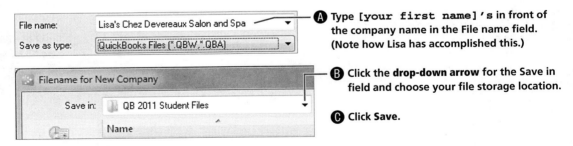

A Type [your first name]'s in front of the company name in the File name field. (Note how Lisa has accomplished this.)

B Click the **drop-down arrow** for the Save in field and choose your file storage location.

C Click **Save**.

Ask your instructor or review Storing Your Exercise Files (located in the student resource center) to learn more about choosing a default storage location for your files.

12. Click the **Go to Setup** button.

A large "Let's get you set up!" window will appear that can guide you through setting up customers, vendors, employees, items, and bank accounts. We will be doing this in the next three lessons, so we will not use this feature right now.

13. Click **Start working**.

You will now see the Quick Start Center displayed over the QuickBooks Home page in the QuickBooks window.

14. Click the **Close** button of the Quick Start Center window, being careful not to click the Close button for the QuickBooks program window.
You will learn a little more about the Quick Start Center later in this lesson. The QuickBooks Home page is now displayed. Leave it open and continue to the next topic.

2.2 Editing Your QuickBooks Preferences

The way you interact with QuickBooks is controlled by the preferences you select. The Preferences window has twenty-one categories of preferences you can set or modify so Quick-Books can work more efficiently for your company.

Notice the two tabs at the top of the window. They allow you to switch between company and personal preferences with a click of the mouse.

Along the left side of the Preferences window you can see the twenty-one preference categories.

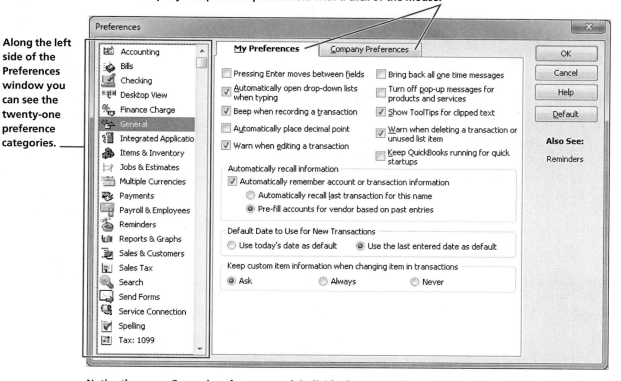

Notice the many General preferences each individual user can choose. Each option will affect how the individual interacts with QuickBooks.

Company vs. Personal Preferences

Each category has two tabs on which changes to preferences can be set: the Company Preferences tab and the My Preferences (personal) tab. Company preferences are controlled by the administrator. They determine how the entire company interacts with QuickBooks. Personal preferences are controlled by each individual user. They dictate interactions between QuickBooks and that one user only.

The following illustrations show an example of a company and a personal preference.

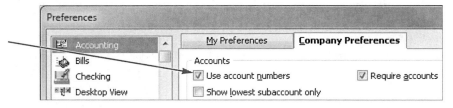

When the administrator makes a change to the company preference, the change will affect how all users interact. In this example, the administrator turned on the preference to use account numbers. In the Chart of Accounts, there would then be an account number associated with each account.

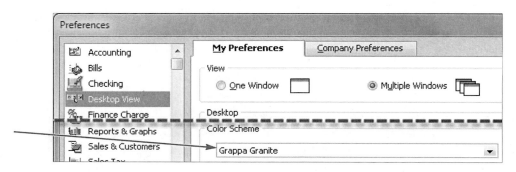

In this example, a user can make a change to the color scheme on the My Preferences tab that will affect only her individual QuickBooks user login.

Using Account Numbers

Many businesses use account numbers for the accounts in their Chart of Accounts. You will be using account numbers as you work with the company file for Chez Devereaux Salon and Spa. Account numbers are somewhat standard within the accounting world. "Somewhat" means that each account type begins with the same number, but the accounts listed within the account type are not universally numbered. Examine the following table to understand how account numbers work. Note that account numbers have a minimum of four characters, and you can use five or six. For instance, a Checking account (which is an asset) could be numbered 1000, 10000, or 100000. This book will use five-digit account numbers.

Account number starts with:	Type of account	Example
1	Asset	Checking Account
2	Liability	Accounts Payable
3	Equity	Retained Earnings
4	Income	Retail Product Sales

Account number starts with:	Type of account	Example
5	Cost of Goods Sold	Purchases – Resale Items
6	Expenses	Utilities Expense
7	Other Income	Interest Income
8	Other Expense	Sales Tax Penalty

Changing the Color Scheme

The default color scheme is sea green. You can change this on the My Preferences tab of the Desktop View category. There are many color schemes available, and you can change your color scheme at any time.

QUICK REFERENCE	EDITING BASIC QUICKBOOKS PREFERENCES
Task	**Procedure**
Edit QuickBooks file preferences	■ Choose Edit→Preferences from the menu bar.
	■ Click the category (listed on the left side of the window) in which you wish to make a change.
	■ Choose either the Company Preferences or My Preferences tab.
	■ Make any necessary changes.
	■ Click OK to save the new preferences.

DEVELOP YOUR SKILLS 2.2.1
Change Your Preferences

In this exercise, you will turn on the account number preference for the company and change the color scheme personal preference.

Turn On the Account Numbers Company Preference

Whether to turn on the use of account numbers is a company preference, is set by the company administrator, and cannot be changed by other users.

1. Choose **Edit→Preferences** from the menu bar.

2. Follow these steps to turn on the account numbers preference:

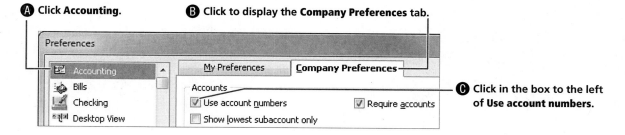

Ⓐ **Click Accounting.**　　Ⓑ **Click to display the Company Preferences tab.**

Ⓒ **Click in the box to the left of Use account numbers.**

The Show lowest subaccount only preference will be introduced in QuickBooks Pro 2011: Level 2.

3. Click **OK** to accept the new preference.

Change a Desktop View Personal Preference

In this section, you will change the color scheme.

4. Choose **Edit→Preferences** from the menu bar.

5. Follow these steps to change your color scheme personal preference:

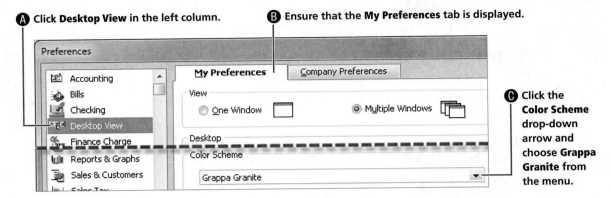

A Click **Desktop View** in the left column.   **B** Ensure that the **My Preferences** tab is displayed.

C Click the **Color Scheme** drop-down arrow and choose **Grappa Granite** from the menu.

6. Click **OK** to accept the new preference.
   Take a look at the icon bar and notice the new purple color scheme displayed. Leave the QuickBooks window open and continue with the next topic.

2.3 Customizing a Company File

During the setup process, QuickBooks allows you to choose a business type similar to your own. It is up to you to take this generic file and customize it to fit your company.

Modifying the Lists in a New File

You will need to look at several lists after you set up your new QuickBooks company to ensure they are correct. If any of them are incorrect or incomplete, you will need to edit, delete, or add entries to them. These lists include the following.

- The Chart of Accounts
- The Customer & Job List
- The Vendor List
- The Item List
- Customer & Vendor Profile Lists
- The Fixed Asset Item List
- The Employees List
- The Payroll Items List
- The Price Level List

Entries in these lists can be created during the EasyStep interview. If you choose to skip the interview, you will need to populate these lists once the company has been created.

The Chart of Accounts

The Chart of Accounts is composed of all of the asset, liability, equity, income, and expense accounts your company utilizes. You use the Chart of Accounts list window to create new accounts, edit existing accounts, and delete unused accounts.

Customizing the Chart of Accounts

The first task you have with your new company file is to fine-tune your Chart of Accounts. If you are using QuickBooks for an existing business, you will want to talk to your accountant and get a copy of your current Chart of Accounts. If you are starting a new business, you may also want to contact your accountant for guidance on how best to set up your Chart of Accounts for your unique company.

Adding Accounts

When you add an account to the Chart of Accounts, make sure to select the correct account type, as this is one of the most prevalent errors accountants find in their clients' QuickBooks files. Keep in mind that your "behind the scenes" action will be incorrect if the wrong account type is selected.

To Edit or Delete—That Is the Question...

The generic Chart of Accounts that QuickBooks provides will have some accounts you probably won't need for your unique business. You can choose to either rename (edit) these accounts or delete them. Renaming an account is appropriate if you are working with the same account type. Deleting is appropriate if you no longer need additional accounts of the same type.

Moving and Sorting Accounts Within the List

You can change the order in which accounts appear within your Chart of Accounts. By default, QuickBooks alphabetizes accounts by type. The Chart of Accounts is structured so that assets are listed first, liabilities second, equity accounts third, income accounts fourth, cost of goods sold accounts fifth, and expense accounts last. This structure must remain intact; you can only move accounts around within their own type.

If you move your accounts and later decide you want them alphabetized by type once again, QuickBooks allows you to resort the list. Resorting the list restores the QuickBooks default.

Subaccounts

To keep precise records, you may wish to use QuickBooks subaccounts. For instance, to keep the number of expense accounts within reason, you are likely to utilize only one telephone expense account for all of your telephone lines. To track expenses more closely, though, you may want to have separate accounts for your office phone, office fax, and cellular phone. Subaccounts are a great way to track these separate expenses while keeping the number of expense accounts down.

When you run Profit & Loss reports and budgets, you have the option to expand the report (show subaccounts) to show detail or collapse the report (show only main accounts) for brevity.

Using Classes in QuickBooks

Classes allow you to track income and expenses for one specific aspect of your company, and they are not tied to any particular customer, job, vendor, or item. For right now, understand that if you choose to use classes for your own business, the best option is to set them up when you create your new company file.

Task	Procedure
Add an account	▪ Open the Chart of Accounts. ▪ Click the Account menu button, and then choose New. ▪ Choose the correct account type, and then click Continue. ▪ Enter all necessary information. ▪ Click Save & Close or Save & New, depending on whether you have additional accounts to create.
Edit an account	▪ Open the Chart of Accounts, and then single-click the account you wish to edit. ▪ Click the Account menu button, and then choose Edit. ▪ Make any necessary changes, and then click Save & Close.
Delete an account	▪ Open the Chart of Accounts, and then single-click the account you wish to delete. ▪ Click the Account menu button. ▪ Choose Delete from the menu; click OK to confirm the deletion.
Create a subaccount	▪ Open the Chart of Accounts. ▪ Click the main account for which you wish to create a subaccount. ▪ Click the Account menu button, and then choose New. ▪ Choose the correct account type, and then click Continue. ▪ Type the name of the subaccount. ▪ Click in the box to the left of Subaccount of. ▪ Click the drop-down arrow, select the main account from the list, and then click OK to create the new subaccount.
Move an account	▪ Open the Chart of Accounts. ▪ Click the account you want to move. ▪ Place your mouse pointer over the diamond to the left of the account name until you see a four-way arrow. ▪ Click and drag the account to the new location within the same account type.
Re-sort accounts	▪ Open the Chart of Accounts. ▪ Click the Account menu button. ▪ Choose Re-sort from the list.

Make the File Fit Your Business

In this exercise, you will take the generic Chart of Accounts created for Chez Devereaux Salon and Spa and make it fit the needs of the company.

Add an Account to the Chart of Accounts

FROM THE KEYBOARD

Ctrl+a to open the Chart of Accounts

The first task is to add an account that Lisa needs but that was not provided in the generic Chart of Accounts, Checking.

1. Click the **Chart of Accounts** task icon in the Company area of the Home page.
   QuickBooks opens the generic Chart of Accounts created for you. Notice the account numbers that you turned on in the previous exercise.

Chart of Accounts

2. Follow these steps to create the new account:

FROM THE KEYBOARD

Ctrl+n to create a new account.

Ⓐ Click the **Account** menu button at the bottom left of the window.

Ⓑ Choose **New** from the menu.

Ⓒ Click in the circle to the left of **Bank**.

Ⓓ Click **Continue**.

Ⓔ Type **10000**.

Ⓕ Tap Tab, and then type **Checking**.

Ⓖ Tap Tab twice, and then type **Silver Falls**

Ⓗ Tap Tab, and then type **11111-44444**.

Ⓘ Tap Tab, and then type **599222043**.

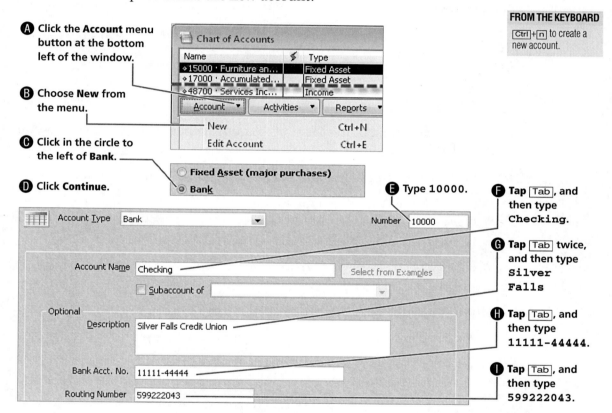

3. Click **Save & Close**.

4. Click **No** in the Set Up Online Services window.
   Take a look at your Chart of Accounts window and notice the new Checking account at the top of the list.

Edit an Account

In Lesson 4, Working with Customers, you will learn how to create items and route them to the proper account in the Chart of Accounts. For now, you will rename the sales account to which you will direct one of the service items.

5. Scroll down the Chart of Accounts, if necessary, and then **single-click** the **Services Income** account.

FROM THE KEYBOARD

Ctrl+e to edit the selected account

6. Click the **Account** menu button, and then choose **Edit Account**.

7. Follow these steps to rename the account:

Ⓐ Click in front of **Services Income,** and then type **Hair.**

Ⓑ Click between *salon* and *services,* and then type **hair.**

Ⓒ Click **Save & Close.**

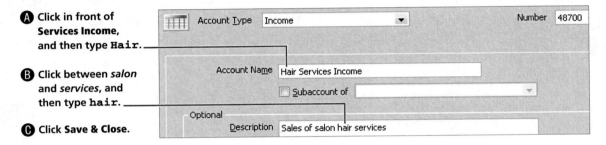

Delete an Account

8. Scroll to the bottom of the Chart of Accounts window, and then **single-click** the **Ask My Accountant** account.

FROM THE KEYBOARD

Ctrl+d to delete the selected account

9. Click the **Account** menu button, and then choose **Delete Account**.

10. Click **OK** in the Delete Account window.

Since you cannot undo an account deletion, QuickBooks verifies that you do mean to delete.

Create Subaccounts

Lisa has decided that she wants to track her telephone expenses more carefully, so she has decided to use subaccounts.

11. Single-click Telephone Expense in the Chart of Accounts.

12. Click the **Account** menu button, and then choose **New**.

13. Follow these steps to create your new subaccount:

Ⓐ Click in the circle to the left of **Expense.**

Ⓑ Click **Continue.**

Ⓒ Type **68110** as the Number.

Ⓓ Tap Tab, and then type **Office Phone.**

Ⓔ Click in the box to the left of **Subaccount** of.

Ⓕ Tap Tab, and then type **t.** QuickBooks will fill in Telephone Expense for you.

Ⓖ Tap Tab, and then type **715.555.4010.**

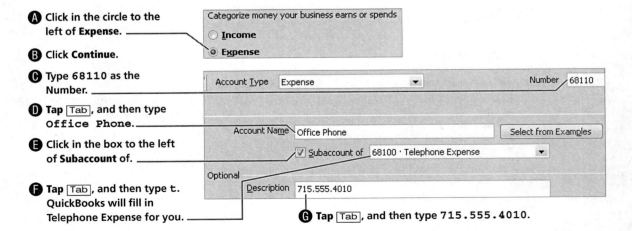

14. Click **Save & New** to add your new subaccount and leave the window open to add another one.

15. Follow sub-steps C–G from step 13 to add the following additional subaccounts for Telephone Expense, clicking **Save & New** after creating the first additional subaccount:

Account Number	Subaccount Name	Description
68120	Fax Line	715.555.4015
68130	Cell Phone	715.555.1011

16. Click **Save & Close** to create the last new subaccount and close the window.

17. Close the **Chart of Accounts** window.

2.4 Working with Opening Balances and Historical Transactions

If you chose a start date for your company that was not the first day you were in business, it is important to enter all of the historical transactions and opening balances in your file.

Entering and Editing Account Opening Balances

You need to make sure that you have the correct opening balances in QuickBooks for all of your accounts. There are five different methods by which you can enter opening balances. The type of account that you are dealing with determines which method, or combination of methods, will work the best. The five methods available are:

- EasyStep Interview (for bank accounts only)
- Journal entries
- Forms (for individual transactions)
- Registers
- Lists (lump sums can be entered when creating entries)

Editing a Beginning Balance

If you need to correct a beginning balance that you entered, you will not be able to do it through the EasyStep Interview or the Edit Account window. In order to accomplish this task, you need to use either the account register or a journal entry. For example, if you incorrectly entered $15,000 as the opening balance for the Savings account when you created it, you will need to open the Savings account register by double-clicking the account in the Chart of Accounts and change the amount in that window.

Entering Historical Transactions for an Account

There are two different ways that you can enter historical transactions into your QuickBooks file. Transactions can be entered either individually or in a summary journal entry.

Entering Historical Transactions Individually

If you wish to enter your transactions individually, you must have all of the data for each one. It is very important that you enter them in the correct order. Check out the following illustration to see the correct order for historical transaction entry.

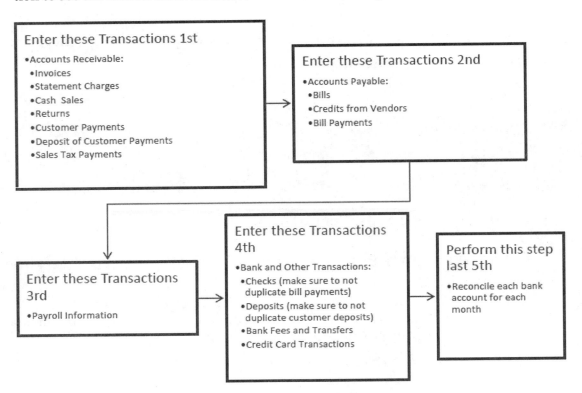

Making a Summary Journal Entry

In a summary journal entry, you will not enter the details of individual transactions; you will only enter the total amounts. In this lesson, you will edit an opening balance in a register.

QUICK REFERENCE	ENTERING HISTORICAL TRANSACTIONS
Task	**Procedure**
Edit an account opening balance	■ Open the register for the account.
	■ Drag to select the opening amount.
	■ Type the correct amount.
	■ Click Record.

Task	Procedure
Enter historical transactions individually	■ Gather the information for all of the historical transactions.
	■ Enter all of your accounts receivable transactions using the proper QuickBooks forms. (Follow the order shown above.)
	■ Enter all of your accounts payable transactions using the proper QuickBooks forms. (Follow the order shown above.)
	■ Enter outstanding payroll information. (For more information regarding payroll, see *QuickBooks Pro 2011: Level 2*.)
	■ Enter outstanding "bank and other" transactions. (Follow the order shown above.)
	■ Reconcile each bank account for each month chronologically.
Make a summary journal entry to account for historical transactions	■ Gather the information for all of the historical transactions.
	■ Determine each account that is affected, whether the net effect is a debit or a credit, and the total amount.
	■ Choose Company→Make General Journal Entries from the menu bar.
	■ Enter each of the affected accounts and the amount of the debit/credit.
	■ Ensure that debits equal credits. (QuickBooks will not allow you to record the journal entry until they do!)
	■ Record the journal entry.

DEVELOP YOUR SKILLS 2.4.1

Deal with an Opening Balance

In this exercise, you will work with a register to deal with an adjustment to the opening balance for the Checking account, since it was not entered when you created the account. Notice that the account that you will credit in this transaction is 30000•Open Balance Equity (the whole account name is cut off due to the size of the field).

1. Click the **Check Register** task icon in the Banking area of the Home page.
   There is only one bank account at this time, so the Checking register will open automatically for you.

2. Follow these steps to enter the opening balance for the Checking account:

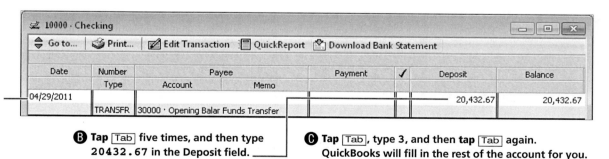

A Type 042911 in the Date

B Tap [Tab] five times, and then type 20432.67 in the Deposit field.

C Tap [Tab], type 3, and then tap [Tab] again. QuickBooks will fill in the rest of the account for you.

3. Click the **Record** button at the bottom of the register window.

4. Close the **Checking** register window.

There will be times when you will need to be able to find answers to questions you have about QuickBooks on your own. QuickBooks has a built-in help feature as well as a "coaching" feature that can come to your rescue in these circumstances.

The QuickBooks "Have a Question?" Window

The QuickBooks "Have a Question?" window, which displays to the right of the main QuickBooks window when open, provides two tabs that allow you to find help.

- **Live Community Tab:** This tab allows you to view questions that have been answered by other users and to ask your own questions of other users.

- **Help Tab:** On this tab, notice the sub-tabs that allow you to view topics relevant to what you are currently doing in QuickBooks or to type a question or keyword(s) in order to search all words in the help topics.

The Live Community feature allows you to interact with other QuickBooks users to give and receive help.

The Back button allows you to return to the previous help topic viewed.

The Print Topic button allows you to print the help topic you are currently viewing.

When using the Search tab, you search all of the words in the individual help topics. In this example, the words "How do I create a company file" will be the subject of the search.

The Maximize, Restore, and Minimize buttons for the main QuickBooks window control the "Have a Question?" window as well.

Once you find the topic you are searching for, QuickBooks allows you to easily print the information by clicking the Print Topic button on the toolbar above the topic title. Or, you can "go green" and save paper by just viewing the topic displayed to the right of your QuickBooks window as you work through the topic.

The Quick Start Center

Earlier in this lesson, you closed the Quick Start Center window that appeared after you created your new company file. This feature is available to you whenever you need it. The button to launch it can be found at the top right of the Home page. This center helps you to perform basic tasks and provides tutorials to help you learn more about working in QuickBooks.

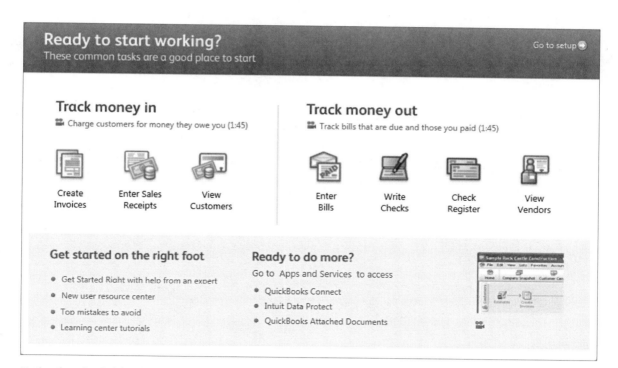

Notice that the Quick Start window is organized in sections to help you track money both coming into and leaving your business. It also features ways to start your QuickBooks experience right and to get more from the software once you are up and running.

QUICK REFERENCE	FINDING HELP IN QUICKBOOKS
Task	**Procedure**
Search for help by browsing relevant topics	■ Choose Help→QuickBooks Help from the menu bar. ■ Click the Help tab. ■ Click the Relevant Topics sub-tab. ■ When you see the topic you desire, scroll down (if necessary) and click it to display the help topic text in the bottom portion of the window.
Search for help by searching the text of the entire help topic	■ Choose Help→QuickBooks Help from the menu bar. ■ Click the Help tab. ■ Click the Search sub-tab. ■ Type the question you have about QuickBooks and then tap [Enter]. ■ Look at the Search results displayed and then click the topic about which you wish to learn more.
Ask a question of another QuickBooks user	■ Choose Help→QuickBooks Help from the menu bar. ■ Click the Live Community tab. ■ Type the question you wish to pose to other users and then click Ask My Question. ■ A web page will launch and then you will need to log in to the Intuit website to post your question. ■ If you feel up to the challenge, you may wish to answer a question for another user as well!

Task	Procedure
Print a help topic	■ Search for the topic of your choice by using either the Relevant Topics or Search sub-tab. ■ Click the Print Topic button on the middle toolbar. ■ Set your printer and print options and then click Print.
Open the Quick Start Center window to view a tutorial	■ Ensure the Home page is displayed. ■ Find and click the Quick Start Center button at the top right of the Home page. ■ Locate and click the hyperlink to the tutorial that will address the topic about which you wish to learn more. ■ A web page will open and your tutorial will be displayed. Close the web page window when you are finished and ready to return to QuickBooks.

DEVELOP YOUR SKILLS 2.5.1

Search for Help

In this exercise, you will use the Search help feature in QuickBooks.

FROM THE KEYBOARD

F1 to open the "Have a Question?" window

1. Choose **Help→QuickBooks Help** from the menu bar, if the "Have a Question?" window is not displayed.

2. Follow these steps to search for a help topic:

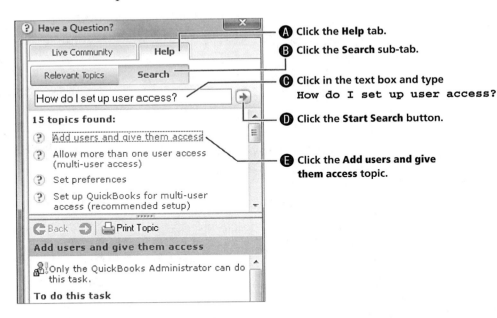

Ⓐ Click the **Help** tab.

Ⓑ Click the **Search** sub-tab.

Ⓒ Click in the text box and type **How do I set up user access?**

Ⓓ Click the **Start Search** button.

Ⓔ Click the **Add users and give them access** topic.

The topic you chose will be displayed in the bottom area of the Help window.

3. Take a look at the bottom section of the "Have a Question?" window, scrolling down if necessary, and read the entire topic.

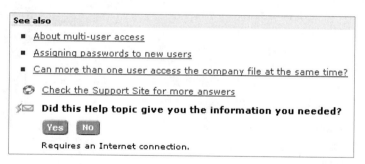

Notice that if you did not find the exact topic you were looking for, QuickBooks provides links to related topics and resources.

4. Click the **Yes** button under the question "Did this Help topic give you the information you needed?"
You can leave the help topic displayed in the "Have a Question?" window and continue with the next section.

2.6 Setting Up Users

When your company grows, and you hire additional employees, you may decide that you need to allow certain employees access to your QuickBooks file.

Administrators and Users

Before you can set up any users for your QuickBooks file, you must set up an administrator who will control the access of all users. You can assign a password for each person with access to your file. The administrator controls all company preferences in the Preferences window. Users have the ability to change only their own personal preferences. QuickBooks allows you to set up unlimited users for your company file, although the number that can access the file at any one time depends on your QuickBooks license agreement.

A user type that was introduced in 2009, the External Accountant, has access to all areas of QuickBooks except those that contain confidential customer information. An External Accountant can conduct reviews of your file and separate the changes from those of other users. Only an administrator can create an External Accountant user.

Restricting Access

When you decide to give employees access to your QuickBooks company file, you may not want them to see all of your company's financial information. You can choose to restrict each individual user's access to specific areas of QuickBooks.

There are nine areas for which you can give access rights to a user. Lisa has asked Bill to help out at Chez Devereaux Salon and Spa with sales and product ordering, so she will need to set him up as a user with limited access. The following illustration displays those areas. In this example, Bill has access to all areas of sales and accounts receivable (creating new transactions, printing forms, and running reports) and can create new purchase and accounts payable transactions.

Access for user: Bill

This user has the following access rights. Click the Leave button to return.

Area	Create	Print	Repo...
Sales and Accounts Receivable	Y	Y	Y
Purchases and Accounts Payable	Y	N	N
Checking and Credit Cards	N	N	n/a
Time Tracking	N	N	N
Payroll and Employees	N	N	N
Sensitive Accounting Activities	N	N	N
Sensitive Financial Reports	N	N	n/a
Changing or Deleting Transactions	Y	n/a	n/a
Changing Closed Transactions	N	n/a	n/a

Setting Passwords

It is very important to make sure you have a password that is not easy for others to guess and yet that is easy for you to remember. Once you set your username and password, the Change QuickBooks Password window allows you to change your password whenever you wish (recommended every 90 days) and to set or change your secret "challenge question" that will allow you to retrieve a forgotten password. This challenge question should not have an answer with which others are familiar.

Working with QuickBooks in a Multi-User Environment

QuickBooks provides a way for more than one user to access a company file at the same time. In QuickBooks Pro and Premier, up to five users can have simultaneous access to the file. Most tasks that you usually do can be completed in multi-user mode, but there are some that must be performed in single-user mode.

You cannot do the following in multi-user mode:

- Create a new company file
- Set or edit a closing date
- Rebuild, clean up, or verify the file
- Create or work with accountant's copies
- Merge, delete, and sort list information
- Change company preferences
- Export and import data

Task	Procedure
Set up an administrator name and password	■ Choose Company→Set Up Users and Passwords→Set Up Users. ■ Select Admin, and then click Edit User. ■ Type the username and password, entering the password twice to verify. ■ Choose a challenge question, if desired. ■ Type the challenge question answer, if necessary. ■ Click OK.
Change an administrator password	■ Choose Company→Set Up Users and Passwords→Change your password from the menu bar. ■ Type a complex password; retype it to verify you did it correctly. ■ Choose a challenge question, if desired. ■ Type the challenge question answer, if necessary. ■ Click OK.
Set up users	■ Choose Company→Set Up Users and Passwords→Set Up Users. ■ Click Add User. ■ Type the username and password, and then click Next. ■ Follow the steps in the "Set up user password and access" screens to customize the access for the user. ■ View the new user's access rights and click Finish.
Switch between multi-user/single-user modes	If you are in single-user mode and wish to switch to multi-user mode: ■ Choose File→Switch to Multi-user Mode from the menu bar. If you are in multi-user mode and wish to switch to single-user mode: ■ Choose File→Switch to Single-user Mode from the menu bar.

DEVELOP YOUR SKILLS 2.6.1
Set Up Users for a Company

In this exercise, you will help Lisa set up Bill as a user for the Chez Devereaux Salon and Spa company file.

Set Up an Administrator and Password

Before Lisa sets Bill up as a user, she needs to set her own password as the administrator.

1. Choose **Company→Set Up Users and Passwords→Set Up Users** from the menu bar.

2. Click **Edit User** to change the name and set a password for the Admin account.

3. Follow these steps to set up Lisa's administrator account and password:

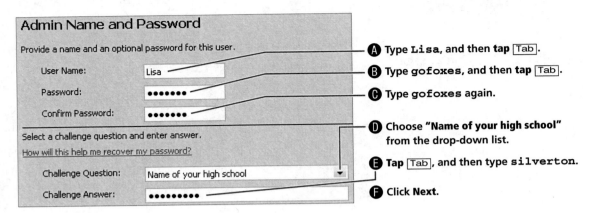

4. Click **Finish**.

Notice that you do not need to change the access areas for the administrator. She has access to everything in the company file!

Add a User

Now that the administrator is set up, you can set up individual users.

5. Click the **Add User** button in the User List window; then follow these steps to add Bill as a user:

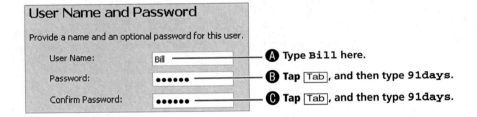

6. Click **Next** twice.

Each time you click Next as you move through the "Set up user password and access" screens, you can change the access for the user in one of nine areas.

7. Click to choose the **Full Access** for Sales and Accounts Receivable option, and then click **Next**.

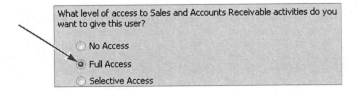

8. Click in the circle to the left of **Selective Access** for Purchases and Accounts Payable.

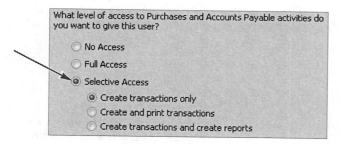

The Create transactions only option will be automatically selected.

9. Click **Finish**; then click **OK** in the Warning window, if necessary.
   Notice that Bill has been added to the User List.

10. Click **View User**.
    You will see a summary of the access you have given to Bill. You can change this at any time by opening the User List, clicking on Bill, and then clicking the Edit User button.

11. Click the **Leave** button in the View user access window.

12. **Close** the User List.

2.7 Closing the Books and Running List Reports

You will not actually close the books yet, but it is important to understand how QuickBooks deals with this task, so it will be covered now. You will, however, find the need to produce list reports early on in your QuickBooks experience. For instance, your accountant may wish to see a list of the accounts you have set up for your business to ensure all is well before you get too far down the road.

Keeping the End in Mind

You are not required to "close the books" in QuickBooks, but you can choose to if you like. When you close the books, QuickBooks:

- Transfers the net income or net loss to Retained Earnings
- Restricts access to transactions prior to the closing date by requiring a password
- Allows you to clean up your data

Only the company file administrator can set a closing date and allow or restrict access to prior-period transactions by user. For now, it is important for you to keep in mind how QuickBooks operates at the end of an accounting period.

The Report Center

There are many preset reports available for you to use in QuickBooks. They are broken into three main categories: list, summary, and transaction. The Report Center is a tool in Quick-Books that allows you to learn about different types of reports without having to create them by trial and error. It includes sample reports and descriptions of the type of information each report provides.

The four tabs at the top of the Report Center window allow you to view the reports that come standard with QuickBooks, the reports you have memorized, your favorite reports, and the reports you have displayed recently.

The main section displays the different available reports. In this illustration, Account Listing is the report selected, and we know from the questions what information it will contain.

Along the left side are the different categories of reports available.

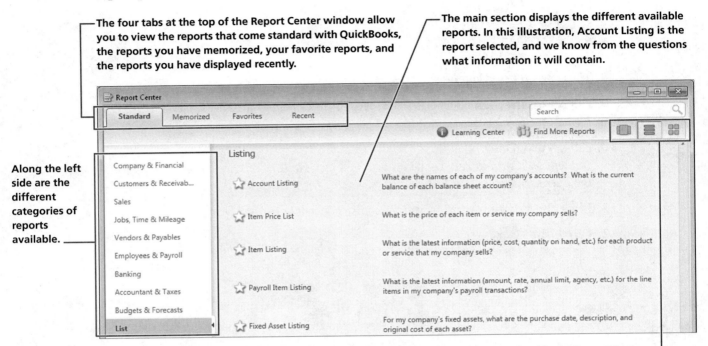

These three buttons allow you to change how you view the information contained in the Report Center.

List Reports in QuickBooks

One category of reports that you can access are list reports. They simply display the information that is found in your various QuickBooks lists in an easy-to-read format.

View Sample Reports Images

An additional feature available in the Report Center is the ability for you to view what a report will look like without having to actually produce the report.

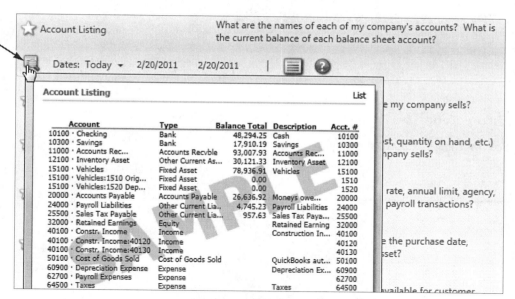

When you place your mouse pointer over the View sample report button, the sample report is displayed for you. To stop viewing the report, simply move your mouse pointer away from the button.

Produce a List Report

In this exercise, Lisa will create a report for her accountant that displays the accounts in her Chart of Accounts.

1. Choose **Reports→Report Center** from the menu bar.

2. Follow these steps to display the report:

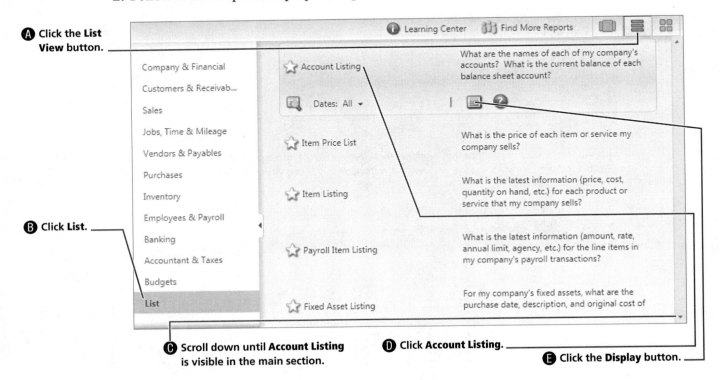

A Click the **List View** button.

B Click **List.**

C Scroll down until **Account Listing** is visible in the main section.

D Click **Account Listing.**

E Click the **Display** button.

A report displaying all of the accounts in your Chart of Accounts is displayed.

3. Close the **Account Listing** report and Report Center windows.

4. Choose the appropriate option for your situation:

FROM THE KEYBOARD
Alt + F4 to exit from QuickBooks

- If you are continuing on to the next lesson or to the end-of-lesson exercises, leave QuickBooks open and move on to the next exercise.

- If you are finished working in QuickBooks for now, choose **File→Exit** from the menu bar.

2.8 Concepts Review

Concepts Review   labyrinthelab.com/qb11_level01

To check your knowledge of the key concepts introduced in this lesson, complete the Concepts Review quiz by going to the URL listed above.

Reinforce Your Skills

Set Up a New QuickBooks Company

In this exercise, you will use the EasyStep Interview to set up the company for the Tea Shoppe at the Lake.

1. If necessary, launch **QuickBooks**.

2. Choose **File→New Company** from the menu bar.

3. Click the **Start Interview** button on the EasyStep Interview screen.

4. Refer to the information on the following page to complete the EasyStep Interview for Susie.

5. Click **Finish** to complete the interview.
   The "Let's get you set up!" window will appear.

6. Click **Start working**.

7. Click the **Close** button on the Quick Start Center window.

Field	Data
Company/Legal Name	**The Tea Shoppe at the Lake**
Tax ID (Federal Employee Identification Number)	99-9999999
Address	316 Swan Drive Lake San Marcos, CA 92078
Phone	760.555.3759
Fax	760.555.3758
Industry Type	Restaurant, Caterer, or Bar
Company Organization	Sole Proprietorship
First Month of Fiscal Year	January
Administrator Password	**Tea4Two** (remember that passwords are case-sensitive)
File Name	**[Your first name]'s Tea Shoppe at the Lake** (e.g. Susie's Tea Shoppe at the Lake)
What Is Sold?	Services Only
Sales Tax	No
Estimates	No
Billing Statements	No
Invoices	Yes
Progress Invoicing	No
Bill Tracking	Yes
Time Tracking	No
Employees	No
Multiple Currencies	No (this option is not available in all versions)
Start Date	**01-31-2011**
Income & Expense Accounts	Start with the accounts provided

Change Preferences

In this exercise, you will change two preferences in the file you just created for the Tea Shoppe.

Before You Begin: *Make sure you have completed Reinforce Your Skills 2.1.*

Turn On the Account Number Preference

You will begin by turning on the account number preference so that when you create and edit accounts, you can enter the numbers.

1. Choose **Edit→Preferences** from the menu bar.

2. Choose the **Accounting** category.

3. Click the **Company Preferences** tab.

4. Click in the box to turn on the **Use account numbers preference**.

5. Click **OK**.

Display Additional Task Icons on the Home Page

Susie would like to be able to create sales receipts in QuickBooks, so you will make the Create Sales Receipts task icon visible on the Home page.

6. Choose **Edit→Preferences** from the menu bar.

7. Choose the **Desktop View** category.

8. Click the **Company Preferences** tab.

9. Click in the box to the left of **Sales Receipts** in the Customers area of the window.

10. Click **OK** to change the preference.

Work with Chart of Accounts

In this exercise, you will add, edit, and delete accounts as well as add subaccounts in the Chart of Accounts.

Add a New Account

Susie wants to add her Checking account.

1. Choose **Lists→Chart of Accounts** from the menu bar.

2. Click the **Account** menu button, and then choose **New**.
   The account menu button can be found in the bottom-left of the Chart of Accounts window.

3. Choose **Bank** as the account type; click **Continue**.

4. Type **10000** in the Number field, **tap** [Tab], and then type **Checking** as the Name.

5. Click **Save & Close**; click **No** in the Set Up Online Services window.

Edit an Account

Susie wants to change the name of the Restaurant Supplies account.

6. Scroll, if necessary, and **right-click** on the **53100•Restaurant Supplies** account; then choose **Edit Account** from the shortcut menu.

7. Change the name of the account to **Shoppe** Supplies, and then click **Save & Close**.

Delete an Account

Susie has decided that she doesn't need the Uniforms expense account, so you will delete it for her.

8. Scroll down, if necessary, and **single-click** on account **68500•Uniforms**.

9. Click the **Account** menu button, and then choose **Delete Account**.

10. Click **OK** to confirm the deletion.

Add Subaccounts

You will now add two subaccounts for the Utilities account: Gas & Electric and Water.

11. Click the **Account** menu button, and then choose **New**.

12. Choose **Expense** as the account type; click **Continue**.

13. Enter **68610** as the Number and **Gas & Electric** as the Name.

14. Make it a subaccount of **68600•Utilities**.

15. Click **Save & New**, and then create one additional subaccount for Utilities: **68620•Water**.

16. Click **Save & Close**; then close the **Chart of Accounts** window.

REINFORCE YOUR SKILLS 2.4

Produce a List Report

In this exercise, you will create an Account Listing report for Susie to show her the work that you have completed on her Chart of Accounts.

1. Choose **Reports→List→Account Listing** from the menu bar.

2. Take a look at the report and make sure that all of the Chart of Accounts work you did in the last exercise is correct.

3. Close the **Account Listing** report.

4. Choose the appropriate option for your situation:
   - If you are continuing on to the next lesson or the rest of the end-of-lesson exercises, leave QuickBooks open.
   - If you are finished working in QuickBooks for now, choose **File→Exit** from the menu bar.

Apply Your Skills

Create and Customize a New Company File

In this exercise, you will create a QuickBooks company file for Dr. Sadie James, DVM. You should use the Skip Interview method to set up the company.

1. Use the following information to set up a new company file for Dr. James.

Company/Legal Name	**Wet Noses Veterinary Clinic**
Tax ID Number	**99-9999999**
Address	**589 Retriever Drive**
	Bothell, WA 98011
Phone	**425-555-2939**
FAX	**425-555-2938**
Income tax form	LLP (Form 1065)
Fiscal Year first month	January
Company Type	Medical, Dental, or Health Service
File Name	**[Your first name]'s Wet Noses Vet Clinic**

2. Click the **Go to setup** button in the Congratulations window.

3. Click **Start working** in the "Let's get you set up!" window.

4. Close the **Quick Start Center** window.

Change Account Preferences

In this exercise, you will set preferences for Wet Noses. You will not turn on account number preferences for this company, as you will operate this company without using them.

1. Open the **Preferences** window.

2. Change the color scheme to **Denim Blues**.

3. Choose to have QuickBooks show the **To Do Notes** when you open the company file.
   Hint: Look in the Reminders category.

4. Choose to turn off **date warnings**.
   Hint: Look in the Accounting category.

5. Close the **Preferences** window.

Modify the Chart of Accounts

In this exercise, you will modify the Chart of Accounts for the company you just created.

1. Open the **Chart of Accounts**.

2. Add two new **Bank** accounts: **Checking** and **Savings**.

3. Add a new **income** account: **Boarding Income**

4. Add a new **expense** account: **Boarding Food and Supplies**

5. Change the name of the Vaccines and Medicines account to **Pharmaceuticals**.

6. Add two **subaccounts** for Pharmaceuticals: **Vaccines** and **Medicines**.

7. Delete the **Uniforms** account.

Answer Questions with Reports

In this exercise, you will answer questions for Dr. James by running reports. You may wish to display the Report Center in List View to help you answer the questions. Ask your instructor if you should print the reports or simply display them on the screen.

1. Dr. James' accountant has asked her if her Chart of Accounts has been set up correctly. Produce a report for her that will show all of the accounts that have been set up for the company.

2. Before Dr. James begins working with customers and vendors, her accountant asked her if the proper terms have been set up for her to use on invoices and bills. Display a report that will show her what terms are currently set up for the company.

3. Choose the appropriate option for your situation:
   - If you are continuing on to the next lesson or the Critical Thinking exercises, leave QuickBooks open.
   - If you are finished working in QuickBooks for now, choose **File→Exit** from the menu bar.

Critical Thinking

In the course of working through the following Critical Thinking exercises, you will be utilizing various skills taught in this and previous lesson(s). Take your time and think carefully about the tasks presented to you. Turn back to the lesson content if you need assistance.

2.1 Sort Through the Stack

You have been hired by Mary Minard to help her with her organization's books. She is the owner of Monkey Business, a nonprofit organization that provides low-income students with help in preparing for college placement exams and applying for scholarships. You have just sat down at her desk and found a pile of papers. It is your job to sort through the papers and make sense of what you find, entering information into QuickBooks whenever appropriate and answering any other questions in a word processing document saved as **Critical Thinking 2-1**.

Following are the notes on the papers you find.

- An email from her accountant: Set up Chart of Accounts, use Non Profit as industry type and add Grant Revenue as an income account.

- A bank statement from Salem First National Bank dated 3/28/2011. Checking account #21375-01, ending balance $5,462.11; Savings account #21375-20, ending balance $18,203.54.

- A handwritten sticky note: Need for three volunteers (Cheryl, Rick, and Susan) to have access to entering donor revenue. How can I make sure they can do this but don't have access to other areas in QuickBooks? Will I need a password or something?

- A scrap of paper with the following written on it: Fiscal year July-June.

- A scribbled phone message from Mary's accountant: Make sure to use account numbers when you set up in QuickBooks.

- The following message on a sticky note: Is there a reminders list to keep me on track???

- Another email from Mary's accountant: Make sure to not have the starting date the day you started the organization...would be too much information to enter. How about 6/30/2011 instead since it is the end of the fiscal year?

- A copy of last year's taxes: Form 990, Federal EIN 99-9999999

- A piece of company letterhead with the following information: Monkey Business 1775 Fidelis Blvd., Salem, OR 97305; Phone 503.555.5239; FAX 503.555.6979.

2.2 Tackle the Tasks

Now is your chance to work a little more with *Chez Devereaux Salon and Spa* and apply the skills that you have learned in this lesson to accomplish additional tasks. Restore the Critical Thinking 2.2 portable company file from your file storage location, and then complete the following tasks. (Remember that the password for the file is "gofoxes"!)

Add Accounts	■ Add the following bank account: 10200•Savings ■ Add the following income account: 48800•Nail Services ■ Add the following expense account: 61500•Client Refreshments
Add Subaccounts	■ Add the following subaccounts to the Utilities account: 68610•Gas & Electric, 68620•Water
Change Account Opening Balance	■ Change the Savings account opening balance to $17,382.35
Search for Help	■ Use the QuickBooks help feature to learn how to enter a bill from a vendor.
Change Preferences	■ Choose to show the Reminders List when opening a company file (hint: Reminders/My Preferences) ■ Turn off the two date warnings (hint: Accounting/Company Preferences)
Create a List Report	■ Create a list report that shows all of the Terms available (these list entries were automatically added when you created the company)

Working with Vendors

LESSON OBJECTIVES

After studying this lesson, you will be able to:

- Work with the Vendor Center and List
- Create and use custom fields
- Understand and use Customer & Vendor Profile Lists
- Enter bills, pay bills, and write checks
- Produce vendor reports and QuickBooks graphs

Tracking expenses properly is very important for your financial statements as well as for keeping your vendors happy! A vendor is essentially anyone to whom you pay money. However, this does not include employees. A vendor could be the electric company, the organization to which you pay taxes, a merchandise supplier, or subcontractors you pay to do work for your customers. QuickBooks allows you to produce 1099 tax forms for subcontractors at the end of the year. In this lesson, you will examine the QuickBooks lists, activities, and reports that allow you to effectively deal with vendors.

Chez Devereaux Salon and Spa

Lisa Devereaux, the owner of Chez Devereaux Salon and Spa, just began using QuickBooks. She needs to work on the Vendor List before she can track her expenses by entering bills, paying bills, and writing checks. Once she has established her list of vendors, she will be able to choose them from drop-down lists in the various vendor forms. Lisa will also learn how to produce reports that will provide relevant vendor information.

Lisa can access the Vendor List and activities (entering and paying bills) from the Vendor Center. In the following illustration you can see the Vendor Center. In total, there are four centers: Customer, Vendor, Employee, and Report. Centers allow you to view a snapshot of information; in this case, it's a snapshot of an individual vendor's information, bills, and payments. You can also initiate a new transaction for the displayed vendor from the center.

┌─ These toolbar buttons allow you to create new list entries,   ┌─ The top-right portion of the window displays
enter new transactions, print a vendor's information, and   information for the vendor you have selected on
export information to Microsoft Excel or Word.   the left, as well as links to reports for the vendor.

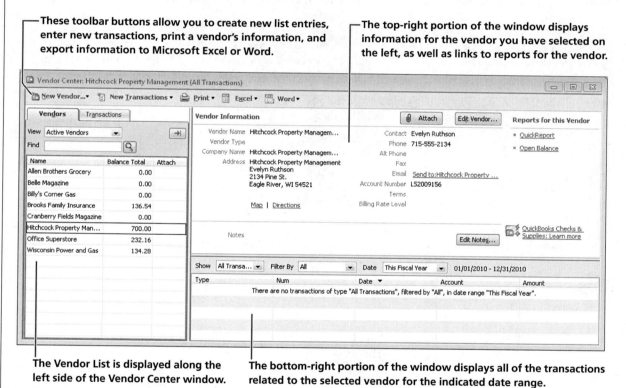

The Vendor List is displayed along the   The bottom-right portion of the window displays all of the transactions
left side of the Vendor Center window.   related to the selected vendor for the indicated date range.

The Vendor Center window displays the Vendor List as well as a snapshot view of the selected vendor.

3.1 Exploring the Vendor Center

In Lesson 1, Introducing QuickBooks Pro, you were introduced to the four types of tasks you would work with in QuickBooks throughout this course. Information is stored in QuickBooks through the use of lists. Lists allow you to store information that can be easily filled into forms by using drop-down arrows or by beginning to type the entry and letting QuickBooks fill in the rest. Lists comprise the database aspect of QuickBooks; the Vendor List can even be exported to contact management software such as Microsoft® Outlook.

Each individual vendor record tracks a lot of information that is organized into two tabs: Address Info and Additional Info. For the information that does not already have a field, you can create Custom Fields to customize QuickBooks for your unique business. Keep in mind that the more information you enter for each vendor, the better prepared you will be later when you learn how to customize reports because you can sort, group, and filter your reports using the information entered into the vendor records. The Vendor List is an integrated part of the Vendor Center.

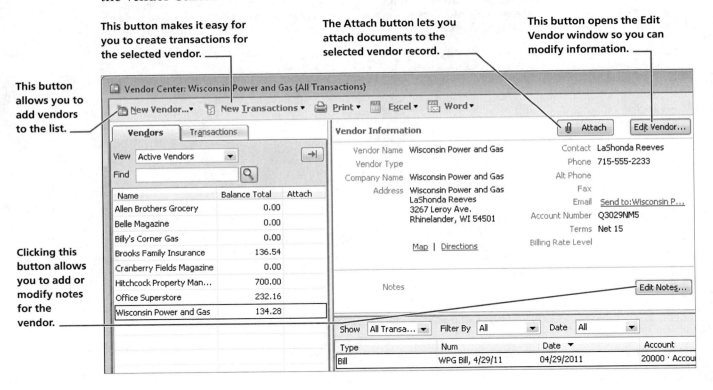

This button makes it easy for you to create transactions for the selected vendor.

The Attach button lets you attach documents to the selected vendor record.

This button opens the Edit Vendor window so you can modify information.

This button allows you to add vendors to the list.

Clicking this button allows you to add or modify notes for the vendor.

Managing the Vendor List

List management tasks are performed similarly for the various lists in QuickBooks. The exact procedure that you follow will depend on whether the list is integrated into a QuickBooks center (Customer & Job, Vendors, Employee) or is accessible via the List option on the menu bar. The lists that are integrated into a center are not accessible separately via the menu bar.

Creating a New Vendor

To start entering vendor transactions, you must first enter your vendors into the Vendor List. You can enter vendors directly into the list, in the Add/Edit Multiple List Entries window (which you will learn more about in *QuickBooks Pro 2011: Level 2*), or "on the fly" in forms such as Enter Bills and Write Checks and then select Quick Add or Setup from the pop-up window. Remember that subcontractors should be set up as vendors, not as employees.

Editing an Existing Vendor

Once created, the vendor can always be edited through the Vendor Center. The only item that cannot be edited after you have created and saved a new vendor is the opening balance (it must be adjusted through the accounts payable register). When you change the information for a vendor, including the vendor's name, it will be reflected in both future and past transactions.

Deleting a Vendor

You can delete a vendor from the Vendor List as long *as you have not used it in a transaction*. If you have used it in a transaction, you can make it inactive, but you cannot delete it until after you close the books for a period and clean up your company's data.

Adding/Editing Multiple List Entries

A new feature that appeared in QuickBooks 2010 is one that allows the customer, vendor, and item lists to all be managed in one location. You can choose to either type the list entries or paste them from Microsoft Excel. In this lesson, you will learn how to enter one entry at a time in the Vendor List. In *QuickBooks Pro 2011: Level 2*, you will have a chance to work with the Add/Edit Multiple List Entries feature.

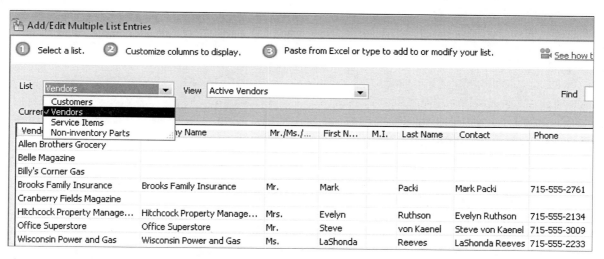

The Add/Edit Multiple List Entries window provides a way for you to quickly add and edit the following types of list entries: Customers, Vendors, Service Items, Inventory Parts (not displayed here because the feature is not yet turned on), and Non-inventory Parts.

Task	Procedure
Edit an existing vendor	■ Open the Vendor Center. ■ Double-click the vendor you need to edit. ■ Make the change(s) to the field(s). ■ Click OK to accept the change(s).
Add a new vendor	■ Open the Vendor Center. ■ Click the New Vendor button on the toolbar. ■ Enter all necessary information. ■ Click OK to accept the new vendor.
Delete a vendor	■ Open the Vendor Center. ■ Click the vendor you wish to delete. ■ Choose Edit→Delete Vendor from the menu bar. ■ Click OK in the window to confirm the deletion.

DEVELOP YOUR SKILLS 3.1.1

Manage the Vendor List

In this exercise, you will restore a portable company file and manage your Vendor List.

Restore a Portable Company File

The first step is to open QuickBooks and restore a portable company file.

1. Start **QuickBooks**.

2. Choose **File→Open or Restore Company** from the menu bar.

3. Click in the circle to the left of **Restore a portable file**.

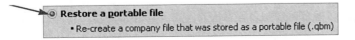

4. Click **Next**.

5. Follow these steps to restore your file:

Ⓐ Navigate to the file storage location you selected when you downloaded the student exercise files from the book website.

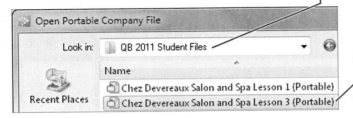

Ⓑ Click to select the Chez Devereaux Salon and Spa Lesson 3 (Portable) file.

Ⓒ Click the **Open** button.

6. Click **Next**; then, follow these steps to determine where the resulting company file will be located:

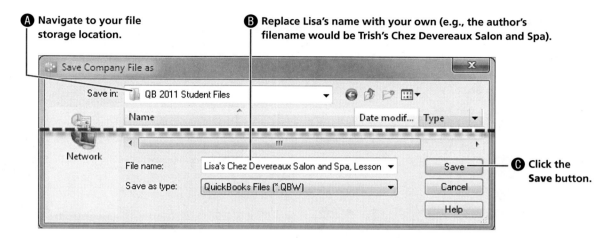

Ⓐ **Navigate to your file storage location.**

Ⓑ **Replace Lisa's name with your own (e.g., the author's filename would be Trish's Chez Devereaux Salon and Spa).**

Ⓒ **Click the Save button.**

It may take a few moments for the portable company file to open. The QuickBooks window opens with the Chez Devereaux Salon and Spa company file ready to go.

7. Click **OK** to close the QuickBooks Information window.

8. Click **No** in the Set Up External Accountant User window, if necessary.

Edit an Existing Vendor

The first step in modifying a vendor record is to open the Vendor Center so you can view the Vendor List.

9. Open the Vendor Center by clicking the **Vendors** button in the Vendors area of the Home page.

10. **Double-click** Brooks Family Insurance to open it for editing.

When you double-click a record on the Vendor List, QuickBooks opens it for editing. You could also single-click the vendor you wish to open and then click the Edit Vendor button.

11. Follow these steps only if the New Feature window is displayed; if it isn't, continue to step 12:

FROM THE KEYBOARD
Ctrl+e to open the selected list item to edit

Ⓐ **Click in this box.**

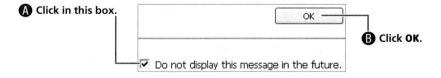

Ⓑ **Click OK.**

12. Change the name in the Contact field to **Reine Dallas**.

In QuickBooks, you can use the same text editing techniques you use in word-processing programs. Simply select the text to be replaced by clicking and dragging the mouse pointer over it and then type the replacement. You can also use the Delete or Backspace keys on your keyboard.

13. Click **OK** to accept the change.

Add a New Vendor

Next you will help Lisa to add a new vendor to the list.

14. Click the **New Vendor** button on the toolbar and choose **New Vendor** from the menu.

15. Follow these steps to enter the address information for the vendor:

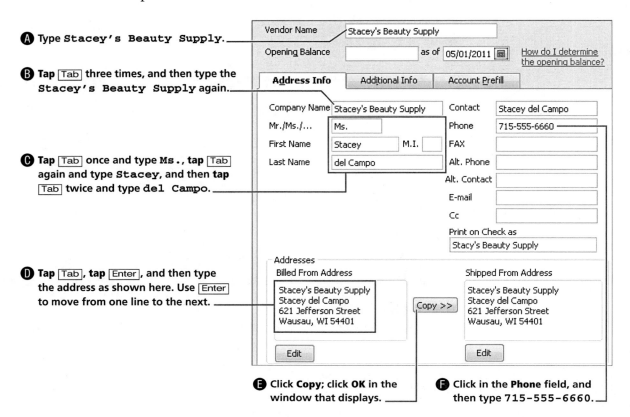

A Type **Stacey's Beauty Supply.**

B Tap [Tab] three times, and then type the **Stacey's Beauty Supply** again.

C Tap [Tab] once and type **Ms.**, tap [Tab] again and type **Stacey**, and then **tap** [Tab] twice and type **del Campo.**

D Tap [Tab], tap [Enter], and then type the address as shown here. Use [Enter] to move from one line to the next.

E Click **Copy**; click **OK** in the window that displays.

F Click in the **Phone** field, and then type **715-555-6660.**

Tapping [Enter] in a field with multiple lines (such as the Billed From Address field) takes you to the next line. Tapping [Enter] while working in a single line field (such as Name or Phone) is equivalent to clicking the default button in the window (the button with the blue highlight around it)—in this case, the OK button.

16. Follow these steps to add the additional vendor information:

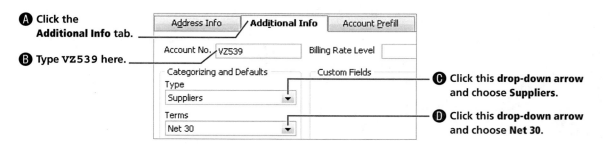

A Click the **Additional Info** tab.

B Type **VZ539** here.

C Click this **drop-down arrow** and choose **Suppliers.**

D Click this **drop-down arrow** and choose **Net 30.**

17. Click **OK** to complete the new vendor record.

Delete a Vendor

Lisa has not purchased anything from Billy's Corner Gas yet, and the company has just gone out of business. You will now delete this company from the Vendor List.

18. **Single-click** the **Billy's Corner Gas** record in the Vendor List to select it.

19. Choose **Edit→Delete Vendor** from the menu bar.
    QuickBooks asks you to confirm the deletion. QuickBooks wants to ensure that you don't delete anything by accident; it will always ask you to confirm deletions.

20. Click **OK** to confirm the deletion.
    In the next step, you will close the Vendor Center window within QuickBooks. Do not click the Close button for the QuickBooks window, as it will exit the program rather than simply close the center window!

21. Close the **Vendor Center** window.

3.2 Working with Customer & Vendor Profile Lists

When you created your new QuickBooks company and chose a type of company on which to base it, QuickBooks gave you a generic Chart of Accounts and populated your Customer & Vendor Profile Lists with entries relevant to your chosen company type. You will see many of these profile lists in the forms and lists you will work with in this book.

Table of Customer & Vendor Profile Lists

Look at the profile lists that QuickBooks provides to track customer and vendor information, as well as the examples of forms and lists in which you may find them appearing as fields.

NAME OF LIST	YOU MAY FIND THIS LIST AS A FIELD ON...
Sales Rep List	■ Customer & Job List (Additional Info tab) ■ Create Invoices form
Customer Type List	■ Customer & Job List (Additional Info tab)
Vendor Type List	■ Vendor List (Additional Info tab)
Job Type List	■ Customer & Job List (Job Info tab)
Terms List	■ Vendor List ■ Create Invoices form
Customer Message List	■ Enter Sales Receipts form
Payment Method List	■ Receive Payments form
Ship Via List	■ Create Invoices form (product or custom template)
Vehicle List	■ Enter Vehicle Mileage window

Making the Lists Work for You

Using the Customer & Vendor Profile Lists can help you in many ways. You can even use a list for a purpose other than that for which it was intended. For instance, your company may not ship products, so you have no need for the Ship Via field. You can use this field to track an additional aspect of your company. You cannot create your own profile list, so you need to maximize the profile lists QuickBooks provides to track all information needed by your company.

The benefit of fully utilizing these lists is that they can be included on reports and custom form templates. This means that if you want to focus a marketing effort on your residential customers, you can create a report and filter out all customer types other than residential.

QUICK REFERENCE	WORKING WITH CUSTOMER & VENDOR PROFILE LISTS
Task	**Procedure**
Open a profile list	■ Choose Lists→Customer & Vendor Profile Lists→[the name of the list you need].
Edit a profile list entry	■ Open the profile list you need to edit.
	■ Double-click the entry you need to edit.
	■ Make any necessary changes, and then click OK.
Create a new profile list entry	■ Open the profile list to which you wish to add an entry.
	■ Right-click within the list and choose New from the shortcut menu.
	■ Enter all relevant information, and then click OK.
Delete a profile list entry	■ Open the profile list from which you wish to delete an entry.
	■ Click the entry to be deleted.
	■ Use Ctrl+d to delete the entry, clicking OK to confirm the deletion.

DEVELOP YOUR SKILLS 3.2.1
Work with Customer & Vendor Profile Lists

In this exercise, you will work with the Customer Message, Vendor Type, and Customer Type Lists. You can use these procedures with any other profile list as well.

Edit a Profile List Entry

1. Choose **Lists→Customer & Vendor Profile Lists→Customer Message List** from the menu bar.

2. **Double-click** "Thank you for your business."

3. **Type** to replace the current message with the following:

   `We truly appreciate your business.`

   When you open the message for editing, the current message is selected (highlighted); it will be replaced when you type the new message.

4. Click **OK** to save the new message.
   Now you can select this message on the Create Invoices and Enter Sales Receipt forms that you will learn about in the next lesson.

5. Close the **Customer Message List** window.

Create a New Profile List Entry

You will now help Lisa to add a new customer type.

6. Choose **Lists→Customer & Vendor Profile Lists→Customer Type List** from the menu bar.

7. Click the **Customer Type** menu button, and then click **New**.

8. Follow these steps to complete the new list entry:

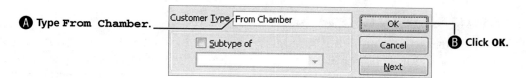

A Type **From Chamber**.

B Click **OK**.

Notice that you can create customer subtypes as well. For instance, if you were a member of two chambers, you could have them listed as subtypes of the entry you just created.

9. Close the **Customer Type List**.

Delete a Profile List Entry

Lisa has decided that she doesn't want to have both Suppliers and Supplies on the Vendor Type List, so you will delete one for her. Since you used Suppliers when you created the vendor entry, you will delete Supplies.

10. Choose **Lists→Customer & Vendor Profile Lists→Vendor Type List** from the menu bar.

11. **Single-click** Supplies.

12. Click the **Vendor Type** menu button and choose **Delete Vendor Type**; click **OK** to confirm the deletion.

13. Close the **Vendor Type List**.

3.3 Creating Custom Fields

You will work with many forms in QuickBooks, and you may choose to send some of these forms to customers and vendors. QuickBooks provides many standard forms (such as invoice, purchase order, and sales receipt), but you can also choose to create your own forms or modify the standard Intuit forms. In order to use custom fields on a form, you must create your own rather than use one of the standard forms provided by QuickBooks.

Adding Custom Fields

Before you can use custom fields in reports, you must first set them up in the lists where they belong. You can set up custom fields for Customers:Jobs, Vendors, Employees, and Items. You can either populate custom fields in the lists or enter the information directly on the forms where they appear.

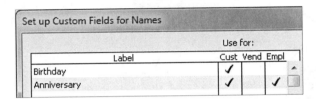

The Set up Custom Fields for Names window allows you to create custom fields for three lists: Customer:Jobs, Vendors, and Employees.

 Custom fields are available for all types of items except for subtotals, sales tax items, and sales tax groups.

QUICK REFERENCE	WORKING WITH CUSTOM FIELDS
Task	**Procedure**
Create custom fields for customers, vendors, and employees	■ Open the Vendor Center (this works the same for the other centers), and then double-click to open a vendor's record.
	■ Click the Additional Info tab, and then click the Define Fields button.
	■ Type the field names.
	■ Click in the column(s) below the list(s) where you want to see each field displayed.
	■ Click OK to close the Set up Custom Fields for Names window.
	■ Enter the new field information into the vendor record.
	■ Click OK to save and close the vendor record.
Create custom fields for items	■ Open the Item List, and then double-click to open an item for editing.
	■ Click the Custom Fields button, and then click the Define Fields button.
	■ Type the labels you wish to use.
	■ Click in the box to the left of each label that you want to activate.
	■ Click OK in the Define Custom Fields for Items window.
	■ Enter any custom field information you want to see automatically appear on forms.
	■ Click OK to close the Custom Fields window, and then again to close the Edit Item window.

Create and Fill Custom Fields

In this exercise, you will help Lisa create custom fields to track additional information and for her to use on custom templates in the future.

Create and Fill Custom Fields

1. Choose **Customers→Customer Center** from the menu bar.

2. **Double-click** Holly Rose in the Customers & Jobs List at the left.

3. Click the **Additional Info** tab.

4. Click the **Define Fields** button in the Custom Fields section of the window.

5. Follow these steps to set up two custom fields:

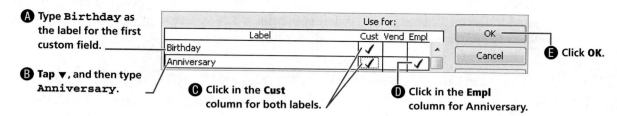

- **A** Type **Birthday** as the label for the first custom field.
- **B** Tap ▼, and then type **Anniversary**.
- **C** Click in the **Cust** column for both labels.
- **D** Click in the **Empl** column for Anniversary.
- **E** Click **OK**.

QuickBooks may display an information window indicating that you can use the custom fields in templates.

6. Click **OK** to acknowledge the prompt, if necessary.

7. Click in the **Birthday** field and type **5/21/69**.

8. Click **OK** to accept the changes and close the Edit Customer window.

9. Close the **Customer Center** window.

Create and Fill an Item Custom Field

You will now add a custom field for items and use it on a non-inventory item.

10. Choose **Lists→Item List** from the menu bar.

11. **Double-click** Hairspray.
    The Edit Item window will open for Hairspray.

12. Click the **Custom Fields** button. Click **OK** to continue to the Custom Fields for Hairspray window if QuickBooks displays an Information window.

13. Click the **Define Fields** button.

14. Follow these steps to add the custom field:

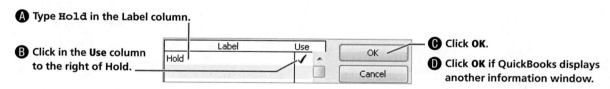

- **A** Type **Hold** in the Label column.
- **B** Click in the **Use** column to the right of Hold.
- **C** Click **OK**.
- **D** Click **OK** if QuickBooks displays another information window.

15. Click **OK**.

QuickBooks closes the Custom Fields for Hairspray window. You did not type in a "hold" here because you will add it to the individual forms instead. If you wish, you can type the custom field information into the Custom Fields for Hairspray window and have it appear on each form or report you create that displays the field.

16. Click **OK** to close the Edit Item window.

17. Close the **Item List**.

3.4 Entering Bills

Once you have set up your initial Vendor List, you can begin to enter spending transactions. In this section, you will learn to enter bills and use accounts payable, which is the account credited when bills are entered. When you enter a bill, you *must* specify a vendor because accounts payable will be credited by the transaction.

Entering Vendor Information on Bills

After you select your vendor from the drop-down list at the top of the form, QuickBooks automatically fills the relevant information for that vendor into the appropriate fields on the Enter Bills window. If you wish to enter a bill for a new vendor not yet entered into the Vendor List, QuickBooks will allow you to create the new record "on the fly."

When entering bills, you need to decide if the expenditure is for an expense or items that you will add to your inventory. The following illustration displays the primary features of the Enter Bills window.

In this lesson you will deal only with expenses. You will learn about QuickBooks' inventory features in *QuickBooks Pro 2011: Level 2*.

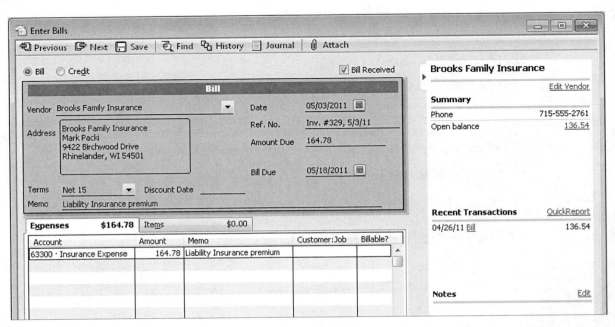

The Enter Bills window. The information displayed on the right shows you a snapshot of information about the selected vendor. Refer to it before you create a new transaction.

When you type a new entry into a field that draws from a list, QuickBooks gives you the opportunity to add the record to the list. When you type a new entry, you can choose to Quick Add the new record (the name will be entered into the list without accompanying information, which you can add at a later date) or to complete a full setup (a window will appear in which you can type all of the relevant information).

Making Changes to Vendor Information on Forms

Whenever you make a change to a vendor's information on a form such as the Enter Bills window, QuickBooks asks if you want to make that change permanent. If you choose Yes, QuickBooks will change the vendor's file. If you choose No, the new information will appear only on the current form; the permanent record remains unchanged.

Allowing List Entries to Fill In

When your insertion point is in a field that draws from a list, you can simply begin to type the entry that you want to choose from the list. QuickBooks will search down the list and fill in the entry for you. This fill-in feature is not case-sensitive, so you can type in lowercase even though the list entry will fill in with the proper capitalization (if you entered it with proper capitalization in the list).

Entering a Vendor "On the Fly"

When you type a new entry into a field that draws from a list, QuickBooks gives you the opportunity to add the record to the list. You can choose to Quick Add the new record (the name will be entered into the list without accompanying information, which you can add at a later date) or to complete a full setup (a New Vendor window appears in which you can type all of the relevant information).

Choosing Accounts to Prefill Information

In QuickBooks, when you set up a vendor, you have the option to choose up to three expense accounts for which information will fill in when you make a payment. By setting up expense account information to be prefilled, you can make tracking expenses easier and faster.

When you enter a vendor's name in the Enter Bills, Write Checks, or Enter Credit Card Charges windows, QuickBooks fills in the expense account names for you. This allows you to then enter the amounts to be debited to each expense account. By prefilling information, you can make sure that you use the same expense account(s) each time you use a particular vendor. You can always choose to override the default accounts that are filled in by changing them in the individual transaction window. If there are fewer than three expense accounts for a vendor, just leave the additional account prefill fields blank.

Passing On Expenses to Customers

When you enter a bill, you may be purchasing equipment or supplies for which you wish to pass on the expense to the customer. QuickBooks allows you to easily indicate which expenses are to be billed to a customer by providing a "Billable?" column in the Enter Bills window. Simply ensure that there is a checkmark in the column; it will be easy to create a customer invoice for the item(s).

The Cost of Goods Sold comprises expenses that are directly related to the manufacture of products or services that the company sells. Some expenses that might be considered Cost of Goods Sold are labor, raw materials, depreciation, and overhead. You cannot pass on the Cost of Goods Sold to a customer (it is instead incorporated into the final price of the product), so make sure that you use the proper type of account (expense) if the costs are to be billed to your customer.

FLASHBACK TO GAAP: COST

Remember that when a company purchases assets, it should record them at cost, not fair market value. For example, if you bought an item worth $750 for $100, the item should be recorded at $100.

Going Behind the Scenes

If you recall in Lesson 1, Introducing QuickBooks Pro, there is a special feature in this book that allows you to take a peek at the accounting that QuickBooks is doing for you when you enter information into forms. Following you will find the first instance of the "Behind the Scenes" feature. Remember that the names used in this feature are the account names Quick-Books uses, not traditional accounting nomenclature. If you would like to learn more about basic accounting principles and what the "behind the scenes stuff" is all about, you may want to check out another Labyrinth Learning book, *The ABCs of Accounting*.

BEHIND THE SCENES

When entering bills, QuickBooks takes care of all of the accounting for you. Here is an illustration of the accounting going on behind the scenes.

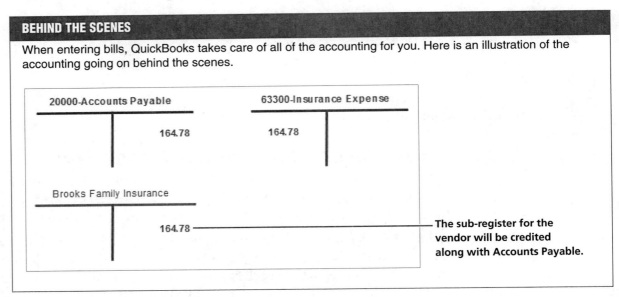

Task	Procedure
Enter a bill for an existing vendor	■ Open the Enter Bills window, and then select a vendor. ■ Enter the amount of the bill, and then ensure that the terms are correct. ■ Expense the bill, making sure to select the correct account(s) on the Expenses tab at the bottom of the window. ■ If desired, select a customer to whom you wish to pass on the expense. ■ Click OK.
Enter a bill for a vendor not on the Vendor List	■ Open the Enter Bills window. ■ Type the vendor's name into the Vendor field, and then choose Quick Add or Set Up. ■ Enter the amount of the bill and the terms for the vendor. ■ Expense the bill, making sure to select the correct account(s) on the Expenses tab at the bottom of the window. ■ If desired, select a customer to whom you wish to pass on the expense. ■ Click OK.

DEVELOP YOUR SKILLS 3.4.1

Enter Bills

In this exercise, you will enter bills and track expenses.

Enter a Bill for an Existing Vendor

First you will enter the insurance bill that Lisa just received into QuickBooks.

1. Click the **Enter Bills** task icon in the Vendors area of the Home page.

2. Click the **Vendor** drop-down button as shown, and then choose **Brooks Family Insurance**.

Look at the form and notice that the vendor's terms fill in for you from the underlying list and that the due date is calculated.

3. Tap `Tab` to move to the date field; then, follow these steps to create a bill for Brooks Family Insurance:

A Type **050311** here.

B **Tap** `Tab`, **and then type** **Inv. #329, 5/3/11.**

C **Tap** `Tab`, **and then type 164.78.**

D **Tap** `Tab` **three times, and then type Liability Insurance premium.**

E **Click in the Account column, and then type i to choose Insurance Expense.**

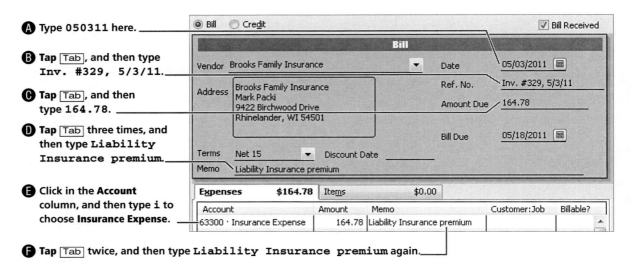

F **Tap** `Tab` **twice, and then type Liability Insurance premium again.**

Notice that when you typed "i," QuickBooks filled in Insurance Expense *from the underlying list for you (in this case, the Chart of Accounts).*

When you type in a date field, you do not need to include the slash marks. QuickBooks will format the date properly for you once you move to the next field.

4. Click the **Save & New** button.

QuickBooks records your bill transaction by crediting Accounts Payable and debiting the expense(s) you chose in the Account column (in this case, 63300•Insurance Expense). The Enter Bills window stays open for the next step.

Enter a Bill for a Vendor Not on the Vendor List

When you enter a vendor name that is not on the Vendor List, QuickBooks allows you to add it to the Vendor List.

5. Make sure the **insertion point** is in the Vendor field at the top of a new bill. Type **Willamina Telephone Company** and tap `Tab`.

A Vendor Not Found window will appear.

6. Click **Set Up**; then, follow these steps to create the new vendor:

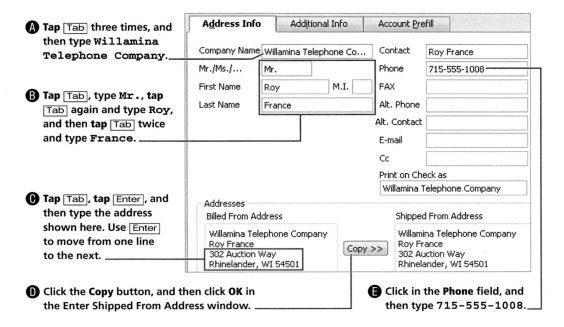

Ⓐ Tap ⎡Tab⎤ three times, and then type `Willamina Telephone Company`.

Ⓑ Tap ⎡Tab⎤, type `Mr.`, tap ⎡Tab⎤ again and type `Roy`, and then **tap** ⎡Tab⎤ **twice** and type `France`.

Ⓒ Tap ⎡Tab⎤, tap ⎡Enter⎤, and then type the address shown here. Use ⎡Enter⎤ to move from one line to the next.

Ⓓ Click the **Copy** button, and then click **OK** in the Enter Shipped From Address window.

Ⓔ Click in the **Phone** field, and then type `715-555-1008`.

7. Follow these steps to add the additional vendor information:

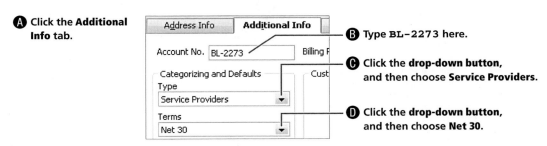

Ⓐ Click the **Additional Info** tab.

Ⓑ Type `BL-2273` here.

Ⓒ Click the **drop-down button**, and then choose **Service Providers**.

Ⓓ Click the **drop-down button**, and then choose **Net 30**.

8. Next, follow these steps to set up an account to prefill for this vendor:

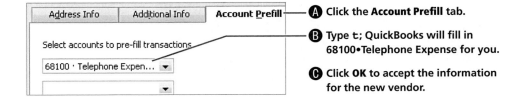

Ⓐ Click the **Account Prefill** tab.

Ⓑ Type `t`; QuickBooks will fill in 68100•Telephone Expense for you.

Ⓒ Click **OK** to accept the information for the new vendor.

9. Finally, follow these steps to finish entering the bill:

Ⓐ Ensure that **05/03/2011** is the date displayed.

Ⓑ Tap ⎡Tab⎤, and then type **Phone bill, 5/2/11.**

Ⓒ Tap ⎡Tab⎤, and then type **129.23.**

Ⓓ Tap ⎡Tab⎤ three times, and then type **Phone bill, 5/2/11.**

Ⓔ Tap ⎡Tab⎤, and then ensure that **68100•Telephone Expense** is displayed.

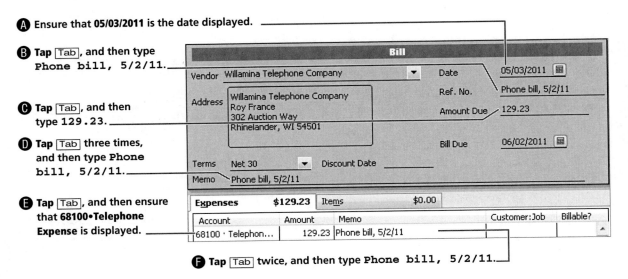

Ⓕ Tap ⎡Tab⎤ twice, and then type **Phone bill, 5/2/11.**

Rather than typing the information for the reference number and memo fields three times, you can drag to select the information in the Ref. No. field, copy it, and then paste it in the two Memo fields.

10. Click **Save & Close** to record the bill.

3.5 Paying Bills

Once you have entered your bills, you will need to pay them in a timely manner. In Quick-Books you use the Pay Bills window to debit accounts payable. The other half of the equation (the account that will be credited) depends on the account from which you withdraw funds (or charge, in the case of bill payment by credit card). The Pay Bills window shows all bills due in chronological order by due date. If you wish, you can choose Due on or before and set a date by which to arrange the list. You also have the option to pay only a portion of what you owe on a particular bill by editing the value in the Amt. To Pay column.

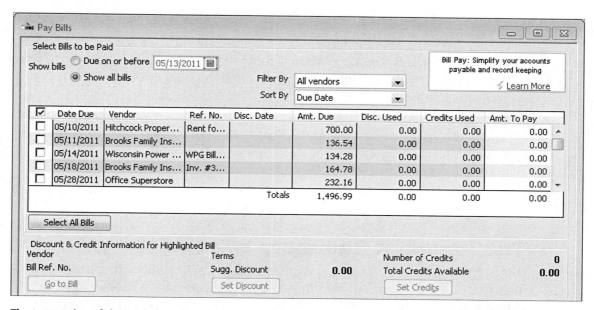

The top portion of the Pay Bills window lets you choose which bills to pay as well as notes any discount and credit information for the selected bill.

 When you have used the Enter Bills window, make sure you use the Pay Bills window to issue the payment—*not* the Write Checks window! If you use the Write Checks window, you will expense the purchase twice and not "clear out" the entry in the accounts payable register.

Payment Details

At the bottom of the Pay Bills window, you must make three important choices regarding your payment: Payment Method, Payment Account, and Payment Date.

QuickBooks allows you to choose the payment options for each bill.

- **Payment Method**—You can choose how you will pay the bill. If you choose to pay by check, you must select whether you will print the check or write it by hand. You will learn how to print checks in the Writing Checks section. You can also choose to pay your bill by credit card. In order to pay by credit card, you must have a credit card account set up. Then you can choose it from the Payment Method drop-down list.

- **Payment Account**—You can select to pay the bill from any bank account you have set up. When you select an account, QuickBooks will show you the ending balance for the account so you can ensure you have enough money to pay the bill. Make sure to select the proper account, as it will be credited behind the scenes!

- **Payment Date**—Make sure you select the date you want the payment to be reflected in your bank and Accounts Payable accounts.

The Payment Summary Window

Once you have chosen to pay the selected bills in the Pay Bills window, QuickBooks will display a Payment Summary window. There are three options made available to you from this window: pay another bill, print checks, or close the window.

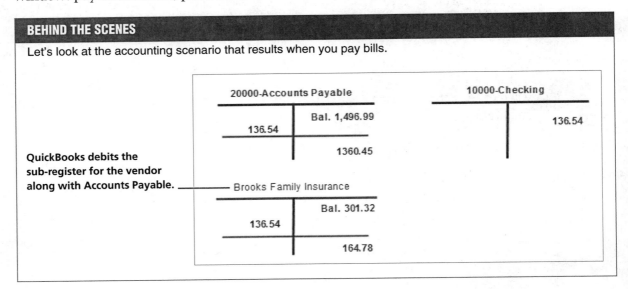

Task	Procedure
Pay a bill	■ Open the Pay Bills window.
	■ Select the bill you want to pay.
	■ Select the account from which you wish to make the payment, along with the payment method and date.
	■ Click Pay & Close or Pay & New, depending on whether you have to pay other bills.
Pay a partial amount on a bill	■ Open the Pay Bills window.
	■ Select the bill you want to pay.
	■ Click and drag over the amount displayed in the Amt. To Pay column and type the amount you will be paying.
	■ Select the account from which you wish to make the payment, along with the payment method and date.
	■ Click Pay & Close or Pay & New, depending on whether you have to pay other bills.

DEVELOP YOUR SKILLS 3.5.1

Pay Bills

In this exercise, you pay bills that have been entered into QuickBooks.

Pay a Bill in Its Entirety

Lisa is ready to pay one of the bills for Brooks Family Insurance. She will complete this task by using the Pay Bills window because the bill was originally entered in the Enter Bills window and, therefore, is "sitting" in Accounts Payable.

1. Click the **Pay Bills** task icon on the Home page.

   The Pay Bills window opens with the Show All Bills option selected at the top of the window.

2. Follow these steps to pay the insurance bill:

A Click in the box beside the bill due on **5/11/11** for **Brooks Family Insurance.**

B Ensure that **Check** is chosen as the payment method.

C Click the calendar button in the Payment Date field, and then click to choose **5/11/11.**

D Ensure that **To be printed** is the option chosen here.

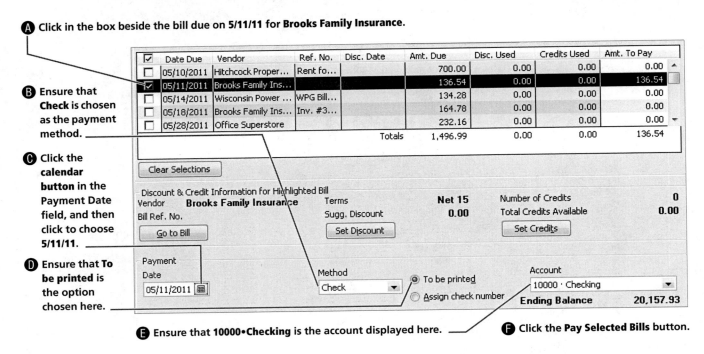

E Ensure that **10000•Checking** is the account displayed here.

F Click the **Pay Selected Bills** button.

3. Click **Pay More Bills** in the Payment Summary window.

Pay a Partial Amount on a Bill

Lisa spoke with her landlord; she made an agreement to pay $500 of the rent due now and the rest in one week. You will help her to pay a partial amount of a bill due.

4. Follow these steps to pay a portion of the Hitchcock Property Management bill:

A Click to place a checkmark for the **Hitchcock Property Management** bill.

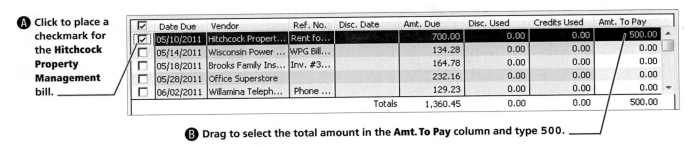

B Drag to select the total amount in the **Amt. To Pay** column and type **500.**

5. Click the **Pay Selected Bills** button to complete the transaction.

6. Click **Pay More Bills** in the Payment Summary window.
Take a look at the current bills to be paid. Notice that the bill for Hitchcock Property Management is still on the list, but only for the remaining amount due of $200.

7. Close the **Pay Bills** window.

3.6 Writing and Printing Checks

If you are using the cash basis of accounting, you do not have to use the enter bills and pay bills features of QuickBooks—even though these are useful features for managing cash flow. Instead, you can simply write a check to pay for your expenditures when they are due and expense them properly.

Remember that if you use the enter bills feature, you must use the pay bills feature for the bills you have entered! If you don't, your expenses will be overstated, and you will have funds "hanging out" in Accounts Payable and getting you into trouble.

As with the Pay Bills window, you must decide from which account to issue the check and whether to print or handwrite the check.

The following illustration displays the primary features of the Write Checks window.

You can choose from which account you wish to write the check (if you have multiple bank accounts).

The number field will display the words To Print if you have chosen the To be printed option or a check number if one has been assigned.

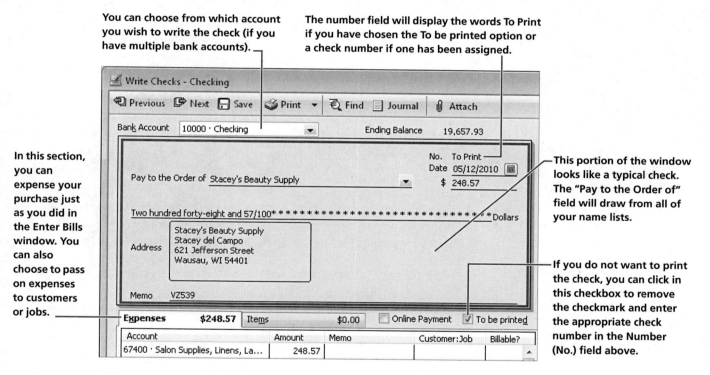

In this section, you can expense your purchase just as you did in the Enter Bills window. You can also choose to pass on expenses to customers or jobs.

This portion of the window looks like a typical check. The "Pay to the Order of" field will draw from all of your name lists.

If you do not want to print the check, you can click in this checkbox to remove the checkmark and enter the appropriate check number in the Number (No.) field above.

Printing Checks

When you choose to print your checks in the Pay Bills and Write Checks windows, QuickBooks will "hold" all of them in a queue until you are ready to print a batch of them. You can issue the command to print a batch of checks from the menu bar, or you can click the Print Checks task icon in the Banking area of the Home page.

FROM THE KEYBOARD

Ctrl+w to open the Write Checks window

Spacebar to check/ uncheck a selected checkbox

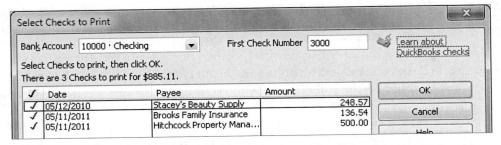

When you choose to print checks, you will see the Select Checks to Print window displayed. You can choose exactly which checks to print in your batch from this window.

BEHIND THE SCENES

The behind the scenes accounting that occurs when you write a check is a hybrid of the two previous transactions (Enter Bills and Pay Bills), with the elimination of Accounts Payable, the middle man.

67400-Salon Supplies, Linens, Laundry		10000-Checking	
248.57			248.57

QUICK REFERENCE	WRITING CHECKS
Task	**Procedure**
Write a check to be printed	■ Open the Write Checks window, and then choose to whom you wish to issue the check.
	■ Type the amount of the check; ensure there is a checkmark in the To be printed box.
	■ Select the proper expense account(s) on the Expense tab; select a customer if you wish to pass on the expense.
	■ Click Save & Close or Save & New, depending on whether you have to create additional checks.
Record a handwritten check	■ Open the Write Checks window, and then choose to whom you wish to issue the check.
	■ Type the amount of the check; ensure there is a *not* a checkmark in the To be printed box.
	■ Type the check number you will be using in the "No." field at the top of the window.
	■ Select the proper expense account(s) on the Expense tab; select a customer if you wish to pass on the expense.
	■ Click Save & Close or Save & New, depending on whether you have to create additional checks.
Print a batch of checks	■ Choose File→Print Forms→Checks from the menu bar.
	■ Select the checks you wish to print from the Select Checks to Print window, and then click OK.
	■ Select the correct options in the Print Checks window, ensuring you have the correct first check number entered, and then click OK.

Write and Print Checks

In this exercise, Lisa will pay for expenses with both printed and handwritten checks.

Create a Check to Be Printed for an Expense

1. Click the **Write Checks** task icon in the Banking area of the Home page.

2. **Tap** [Tab] twice; then, follow these steps to complete the check:

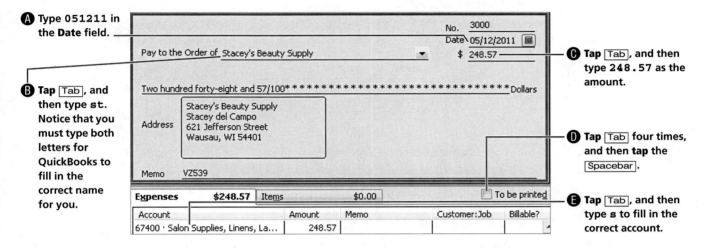

Ⓐ Type 051211 in the **Date** field.

Ⓑ **Tap** [Tab], and then type **st**. Notice that you must type both letters for QuickBooks to fill in the correct name for you.

Ⓒ **Tap** [Tab], and then type **248.57** as the amount.

Ⓓ **Tap** [Tab] four times, and then **tap the** [Spacebar].

Ⓔ **Tap** [Tab], and then type **s** to fill in the correct account.

Notice that QuickBooks automatically fills in the vendor's account number into the Memo field of the check for you.

3. Click **Save & New** to record this check and leave the Write Checks window open.

Record a Handwritten Check

You may not always be at your computer when you wish to write a check. In this situation, Lisa has taken her checkbook shopping and needs to record the handwritten check.

4. Click to remove the checkmark from the **To be printed** box.

Notice that once you remove the checkmark, the next check number appears in the No. field at the top of the check. If this number is not correct, you can select and replace it.

5. Follow these steps to record the handwritten check:

A Ensure **05/12/2011** is the date displayed.

B Tap Tab, and then type
Cost Club.

C Click in the **Pay to the Order of** field, and then choose to **Quick Add** as a new vendor.

D Type 183.46 as the amount.

E Click in the first line of the **Account** column, and then type o.

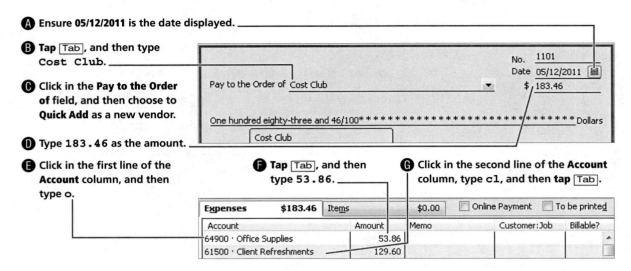

F Tap Tab, and then type 53.86.

G Click in the second line of the **Account** column, type c1, and then tap Tab.

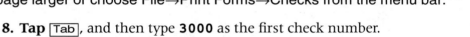

Notice that the expenditure was split between multiple expense accounts and that QuickBooks filled in the amount remaining after you filled in the amount on the first line.

6. Click the **Save & Close** button to complete the transaction.

Print a Batch of Checks

Once you have indicated that checks are to be printed, you need to issue a separate command to print them.

7. Click the **Print Checks** task icon in the Banking area of the Home page.

If you don't see the Print Checks task icon, use the sizing arrow to make the Home page larger or choose File→Print Forms→Checks from the menu bar.

8. Tap Tab, and then type **3000** as the first check number.
By default, all of the checks will be selected.

9. Click the checkmark to the left of the **Brooks Family Insurance** to deselect it.

✓	Date	Payee	Amount
	05/11/2011	Brooks Family Insurance	136.54
✓	05/11/2011	Hitchcock Property Mana...	500.00
✓	05/12/2011	Stacey's Beauty Supply	248.57

10. Click **OK**.
The Print Checks window will appear.

If you wish to be "green," you can choose to not physically print the checks in the next step by choosing to print to PDF or to just preview how they would appear if printed.

11. Ensure that **Voucher** is chosen as the check style and then click **Print**.
QuickBooks will display a Print Checks - Confirmation window. Here you have the opportunity to reprint any checks that did not print correctly or to troubleshoot the order in which your checks printed.

12. Click **OK** in the Print Checks - Confirmation window.

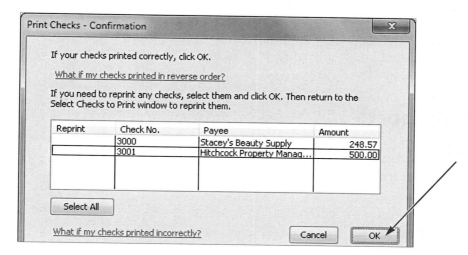

Notice that there are links to help you if your checks do not print correctly.

3.7 Producing Vendor Reports

Once you have recorded your vendor-related transactions, QuickBooks has many reports that you can produce to view your data. In Lesson 2, Creating a Company, you learned about list reports. The other two general types of reports are listed below.

■ Summary reports subtotal your data and provide a summary.

■ Transaction reports show each transaction that makes up the subtotal found in a summary report.

If you wish to see all transactions grouped by vendor, there are two different reports you can run. The Vendor Balance Detail report (found in the Vendors & Payables category) shows only those transactions affecting Accounts Payable (transactions entered and paid as "bills"). The Expense by Vendor reports (both summary and detail, found in the Company & Financial category) show transactions made by all payment methods.

The Report Window Toolbar

The Vendor Balance Summary report toolbar is shown in the following illustration. When viewing other reports, you may also see additional buttons specific to certain reports.

Some of the basic functions that the toolbar buttons allow you the ability to do include:

- Change and memorize the settings for the report
- Print or email the report; clicking the Print button will also allow you to choose to preview how the report will appear in printed form before you issue the command to print it
- Export the report to Microsoft Excel

QuickReports

QuickReports can be run from the various center windows. They show all transactions recorded in QuickBooks for a particular list record. You will use this report to get a quick snapshot of all vendor transactions for Hitchcock Property Management in the Develop Your Skills exercise.

QuickZoom

QuickBooks has a great feature called QuickZoom. This feature allows you to zoom through underlying sub-reports until you reach the form where the data was originally entered. This can be extremely useful if you have questions as to where a figure in a report comes from.

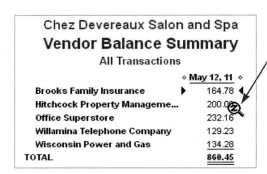

When you see the zoom pointer, you are at a place where you can double-click to dive deeper into your data. The number of layers you have to zoom through before you get to your original form depends on the type of report (or graph) with which you start. For instance, in this figure, if we were to double-click, we would see all of the transactions that have led to the $200 balance for Hitchcock Property Management.

QUICK REFERENCE	CREATING VENDOR-RELATED REPORTS
Task	**Procedure**
Produce a QuickReport	■ Open the center that contains the record on which you wish to run the report. ■ Click the list entry. ■ Click the QuickReport link at the right of the center window. ■ Set the correct date range.
Produce a vendor-related report using the Report Center	■ Choose Reports→Report Center from the menu bar. ■ Choose Vendors & Payables as the report category. ■ Click on the report you wish to produce in the main section of the Report Center. ■ Click the Display report button.
Print or print preview a report	■ Display the report you wish to print or preview. ■ Click the Print button on the toolbar. ■ Choose the option that is appropriate for you: Click Preview to see how the report will look printed *or* click Print to send a copy of the report to the indicated printer.

Produce Vendor Reports

In this exercise, you will produce a vendor QuickReport, a vendor summary report, and a vendor detail report.

Display a Vendor QuickReport

1. Open the Vendor Center by clicking the **Vendor Center** button on the icon bar.

2. **Single-click** Hitchcock Property Management to select it.
   You must always select the list item on which you wish to run a report.

3. Click the **QuickReport** link at the right of the Vendor Center window.
   If you cannot see the QuickReport link, use the sizing arrows to make the window wider.

4. Change the date range to **All** by typing **a** to select All from the Dates list.

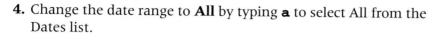

	Type	Date	Num	Memo	Account	Clr	Split	Debit	Credit
Hitchcock Property Management									
	Bill	04/30/2011	Rent...	Rent for May...	20000 · Accounts...		67100 · Rent Expen...		700.00
	Bill Pmt -Check	05/11/2011	3001	LS2009156	10000 · Checking		20000 · Accounts P...		500.00

Chez Devereaux Salon and Spa
Vendor QuickReport
All Transactions

A vendor QuickReport will display all transactions for a selected vendor within a designated date range.

When you first display a report, the Dates field is selected. Typing *a* chooses All from the Dates list.

5. Close the **Vendor QuickReport** and the **Vendor Center** windows.

Create a Vendor Summary Report and Use QuickZoom

You will now create a report that shows what you owe all vendors. Then you will use QuickZoom to see the details of where a balance originated.

6. Choose **Reports→Vendors & Payables→Vendor Balance Summary** from the menu bar.
   You can generate reports through the Report Center or the menu bar with the same result. The report will be displayed with the date range of All selected, as it is the default for this particular report.

7. Place your mouse pointer over the amount listed for Brooks Family Insurance until you see the **zoom pointer**, as displayed in the illustration below, and then **double-click**.

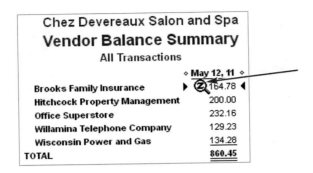

A Vendor Balance Detail report will be displayed that shows the transactions leading to the balance for Brooks Family Insurance. You can also display a Vendor Balance Detail report directly by choosing it from the menu bar or Report Center.

8. Place your mouse pointer over the Bill date 5/3/11 that you entered for this vendor until you see the **zoom pointer**, and then **double-click**.

Chez Devereaux Salon and Spa
Vendor Balance Detail
All Transactions

Type	Date	Num	Account	Amount	Balance
Brooks Family Insurance					
Bill	04/26/2011		20000 · Accounts Payable	136.54	136.54
Bill	05/03/2011	Inv. #329,...	20000 · Accounts Payable	164.78	301.32
Bill Pmt -Check	05/11/2011		20000 · Accounts Payable	-136.54	164.78
Total Brooks Family Insurance				164.78	164.78

The Enter Bills window will open with the bill that you entered for this vendor earlier in this lesson displayed.

9. Choose **Window→Close All** from the menu bar.
   Click No if asked to memorize any of the reports displayed.

Display a Vendor Detail Report

Now you will create a report that lists the details for all of the unpaid bills in Accounts Payable.

10. Choose **Reports→Vendors & Payables→Unpaid Bills Detail** from the menu bar.

11. **Tap** a to set the date range to All.
    The Unpaid Bills Detail report will be displayed, listing the five unpaid bills totaling $860.45.

12. Close the report, clicking **No** when asked if you want to memorize it.

3.8 Working with QuickBooks Graphs

QuickBooks provides several graphs along with the preset reports. QuickBooks graphs are accessible through the Reports option on the menu bar or through the Report Center.

Types of QuickBooks Graphs

Following are the six graphs provided by QuickBooks. If you can't find a graph that suits your needs, you always have the option of exporting a report to Microsoft Excel and using the Excel charting features to create additional charts and graphs.

The graphs provided in QuickBooks include:

- Income and Expense
- Net Worth
- Accounts Receivable
- Sales
- Accounts Payable
- Budget vs. Actual

The Graph Toolbar

The Graph toolbar displays different buttons depending on which graph you have created. Once you have created your graph, you can use the Graph toolbar to do a variety of tasks such as:

- Customize your graph by date
- Choose whether to view your data by account, customer, or class
- View your next group of information
- Print your graph
- Refresh the data contained within your graph (if you have made changes to your data since the graph was created)

For some graphs, there are also buttons at the bottom of the window that allow you to choose how to view the pie chart data at the bottom of the window (e.g., by Income or by Expense).

QuickZooming with Graphs

The QuickZoom feature you used previously in this lesson for reports is also available with graphs. You simply double-click on a portion of a graph (when you see the QuickZoom pointer) to zoom in and see where the data comes from.

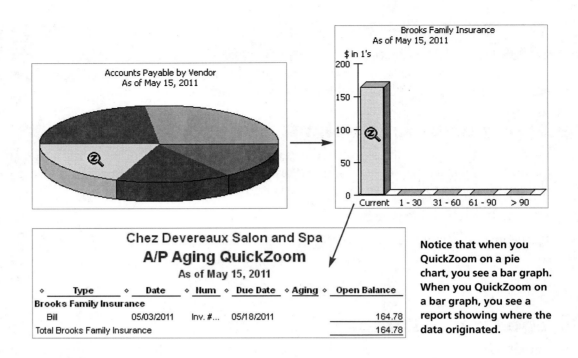

Notice that when you QuickZoom on a pie chart, you see a bar graph. When you QuickZoom on a bar graph, you see a report showing where the data originated.

DEVELOP YOUR SKILLS 3.8.1

Create QuickBooks Graphs

In this exercise, you will create a graph that will depict what is in your Accounts Payable account. You will use QuickZoom to drill down to the source of the data for one vendor.

Create an Accounts Payable Graph

1. Choose **Reports→Vendors & Payables→Accounts Payable Graph** from the menu bar.

2. Follow these steps to set the date for the graph:

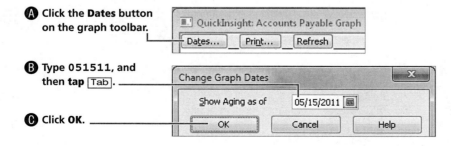

Ⓐ Click the **Dates** button on the graph toolbar.

Ⓑ Type **051511**, and then **tap** Tab.

Ⓒ Click **OK**.

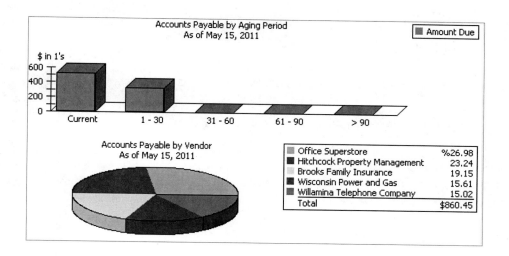

The Accounts Payable graph will be displayed with all balances owing as of May 15.

3. Place your mouse pointer over the **yellow slice** that shows how much of the Accounts Payable balance is owed to Brooks Family Insurance, and then hold down the **right mouse button**. *Notice that holding down the right mouse button will allow you to see the dollar amount corresponding to the "pie slice."*

4. **Double-click** on the pie slice for **Brooks Family Insurance**. *A bar graph will appear showing just the amount for the selected vendor.*

5. **Double-click** on the **bar graph** showing the current amount owed to the vendor. *An A/P Aging report will be displayed.*

6. **Double-click** on the bill dated **5/3/11** for Brooks Family Insurance. *The Enter Bills window will be displayed. This is as far as QuickZoom will go!*

7. Choose **Window→Close all** from the menu bar.

8. Choose **Company→Home Page** from the menu bar.

9. Choose the appropriate option for your situation:

   ■ If you are continuing on to the next lesson or to the end-of-lesson exercises, leave QuickBooks open and move on to the next exercise.

   ■ If you are finished working in QuickBooks for now, choose **File→Exit** from the menu bar.

3.9 Concepts Review

Concepts Review   labyrinthelab.com/qb11_level01

To check your knowledge of the key concepts introduced in this lesson, complete the Concepts Review quiz by going to the URL listed above.

Reinforce Your Skills

Before you begin the Reinforce Your Skills exercises, complete one of these options:

■ *Open the file [Your name] Tea Shoppe at the Lake from your file storage location that you used for Lesson 1.*

■ *Restore the Lesson 3 Tea Shoppe at the Lake file from your file storage location. If you need to review how to restore a portable company file, take a peek at Develop Your Skills 3.1.1. Make sure to place your name as the first word in the company filename (e.g., Susie's Tea Shoppe at the Lake).*

REINFORCE YOUR SKILLS 3.1
Manage the Vendor List

In this exercise, you will work with the Vendor List for the Tea Shoppe at the Lake. You will edit an existing vendor, create a new vendor, and delete a vendor.

Edit a Vendor Record

Valley Insurance Company has changed its name to Vista Insurance Company, so you will help Susie to make that change in QuickBooks.

1. Open the Vendor Center by choosing **Vendors→Vendor Center** from the menu bar.

2. **Double-click** Valley Insurance Company to open it for editing.

3. Change the vendor's name to **Vista Insurance Company**.
   You will have to change the name in five separate places. This new name will be reflected in all transactions that deal with this vendor—past and present.

4. Click **OK** to accept the change.

Add a New Vendor

Susie has decided to start selling some new candies that she has discovered. You will set up the company as a vendor.

5. Click the **New Vendor** button, and then choose **New Vendor**.

6. Enter the following information to create a new vendor:

Company Name	**Carmela's Old Fashioned Candies**
Contact Name	**Ms. Carmela Hutch**
Address	**525 E. San Marcos Road**
	San Marcos, CA 92069
Phone	**760-555-9438**
Fax	**760-555-9455**
Type	Suppliers
Terms	Net 15
Account #	**84-976**

7. Click **OK** to accept the new vendor record.

Delete a Vendor

8. Click **Carlsbad Restaurant Supply** to select it.

9. Choose **Edit→Delete Vendor** from the menu bar.

10. Click **OK** to confirm the deletion.

11. Close the **Vendor Center** window.

Create and Populate Custom Fields

In this exercise, you will create and populate a custom field.

1. Choose **Customers→Customer Center** from the menu bar.

2. **Double-click** to open **Suzanne Stevens** for editing.

3. Click the **Additional Info** tab, and then click the **Define Fields** button.

4. Type **Favorite Drink** as a label, and then place a check in the **Cust** column to the right of the label.

5. Click **OK** twice to accept the new custom field.

6. Click in the **Favorite Drink Custom Field** for Suzanne, and then type **Soy latte w/ honey**.

7. Click **OK** to close the Edit Customer window.

8. Close the **Customer Center**.
   The custom field will now be available for all customers.

Enter and Pay Bills

In this exercise, you will enter a bill Susie just received. You will also pay all bills due by a certain date for Susie.

Enter a Bill

1. Open the Enter Bills window by choosing **Vendors→Enter Bills** from the menu bar.

2. Click the **drop-down arrow** and choose **San Marcos Gas & Electric** as the Vendor.

3. Set the date to **5/19/2011**.

4. Type **$173.54** as the amount, and choose **Utilities** as the account.

5. Click the **Save & Close** button to enter the transaction and close the window.

Pay a Bill

6. Open the Pay Bills window by choosing **Vendors→Pay Bills** from the menu bar.

7. Choose all bills that are due on or before **5/21/2011** (you should find four).

8. Set the date to **5/21/11**, and choose to print the checks.

9. Click **Pay Selected Bills** to record the payments and close the window.

10. Click **Done** in the Payment Summary Window.

Write and Print Checks

In this exercise, you will write a check for an expense and print the checks you have created.

Use the Write Checks Window to Enter an Expense

1. Open the Write Checks window by choosing **Banking→Write Checks** from the menu bar.

2. Set the check number to be **printed**.

3. Set the date to **5/20/2011**.

4. Type **San Diego County** into the Pay to the Order of field and choose to **Quick Add** it to the Vendor List.

5. Type **$125** as the amount and **Business License** as the memo.

6. Select **Business Licenses and Permits** as the account.

7. Choose **Save & Close** to accept the transaction and close the window.

Print a Batch of Checks

8. Choose **File→Print Forms→Checks** from the menu bar.

Notice that, by default, QuickBooks selects all checks; you can change this if you need to.

9. Ensure that **Checking** is the bank account chosen; then, verify that **1104** is the first check number.

10. Click **OK** to move to the Print Checks window.

At this point you can verify that the correct printer and check style are selected. For exercise purposes, you will "stay green" and not print the checks—unless your instructor asks you to do so.

11. Click **Cancel** in both windows.

REINFORCE YOUR SKILLS 3.5

Create Vendor Reports

In this exercise, you will run a vendor report for the Tea Shoppe.

Run a Vendor-Related Report

1. Choose **Reports→Vendors & Payables→Transaction List by Vendor** from the menu bar.

2. Set the date range to **All**.

3. Choose **Window→Close All** from the menu bar.

4. Choose the appropriate option for your situation:

- If you are continuing on to the next lesson or the rest of the end-of-lesson exercises, leave QuickBooks open.

- If you are finished working in QuickBooks for now, choose **File→Exit** from the menu bar.

Apply Your Skills

Before you begin these exercises, restore the Wet Noses Lesson 3 (Portable) file. Name the file [Your Name]'s Wet Noses Vet Clinic. If you need to review how to restore a portable company file, follow steps 1–8 in Develop Your Skills 3.1.1.

APPLY YOUR SKILLS 3.1

Work with the Vendor List and Vendor Type List

In this exercise, you will manage the Vendor List for Wet Noses.

1. Using the following information, create three new **Vendor List** entries.

Name	Casey's Consulting	Take a Walk	Billy's Van Service
Address	902 Creekview Dr. Kirkland, WA 98034	13602 75th Ave NE Seattle, WA 98132	9501 NE 182nd Pl Bothell, WA 98011
Phone	425-555-9569	206-555-9433	425-555-4477
Fax	425-555-9568	206-555-9434	425-555-4478
Contact Name	Ms. Casey Scripps	Ms. Shannon High	Mr. Billy Ranch
Type	Consultant	Service Provider	Service Provider
Terms	Due on Receipt	Net 15	Net 15
Account Number	JR154	VET87	BB23

2. Edit the **Puget Sound Power Company** vendor record to display **Shaunda Jones** as the contact.

3. Add the following vendor types to the existing vendor records, adding a new entry to the **Vendor Type List** when necessary:

   ■ Wyland Broadband: Service Providers
   ■ Northshore Water Company: Utilities
   ■ Oberg Property Management: Service Providers
   ■ Puget Sound Power Company: Utilities
   ■ Seattle Vet Supply: Suppliers
   ■ Whoville Office Supplies: Supplies
   ■ Brian's Pet Taxi: Service Providers

Create Custom Fields

In this exercise, you will create a custom field and populate it for customers.

1. Open the **Customer Center**.

2. **Double-click** Becky Karakash:Dog-Spencer for editing, and then click the **Additional Info** tab.

3. Click the **Define Fields** button.

4. Add the following **Labels** for Customers: **Species**, **Breed**, **Color**, and **Gender**.

5. Click **OK** twice to add the new custom fields.

6. Fill in the custom fields for Spencer using the following information:
   - Species: **Canine**
   - Breed: **Golden Retriever**
   - Color: **Light Brown**
   - Gender: **Male**

7. Click **OK** to close the Edit Job window.

8. Close the **Customer Center**.

Perform Vendor Transactions

In this exercise, you will deal with expenses incurred by Wet Noses.

Enter and Pay Bills

1. On 7/2/2011, Dr. James received a bill from Seattle Vet Supply for $3,813.58. It should be broken down by account as follows: $1,773.25 for medical supplies, $1,056.92 for vaccines, and $983.41 for medicines.

2. Enter a bill received on 7/8/2011 from Northshore Water Company for **$210.67**.

3. On 7/18/2011, a bill was received from Puget Sound Power Company for **$241.33**.

4. Enter a bill received on 7/21/2011 from Wyland Broadband for **$159.44**. It should be broken down by account as follows: $55.99 for Internet service and $103.45 for Telephone service.

5. On 7/21/2011, Sadie decided to sit down and pay her bills. Pay all of the bills due on or before 7/22/2011. You will print the checks later.

6. Choose **Done** in the Payment Summary window.

Write and Print Checks

7. Dr. James took all of her employees out for a working lunch at Laura's Café on 7/11/2011. The total cost was **$84.35**. She wrote a check at the restaurant, using check number 1418.

8. Print all of the checks in the queue waiting to be printed, using 1419 as the first check number.

Answer Questions with Reports

In this exercise, you will answer questions for Dr. James by running reports. You may wish to display the Report Center in List View to help you answer the questions. Ask your instructor if you should print the reports or simply display them on the screen.

1. Are any of the bills overdue?

2. Is there a way to see all of the transactions for each vendor?

3. I would like to have a list of the phone numbers for all of the vendors. Can you create one for me?

4. What is the amount owed to each vendor and what transactions make up each balance?

5. Choose the appropriate option for your situation:

   ■ If you are continuing on to the next lesson or the Critical Thinking exercises, leave QuickBooks open.

   ■ If you are finished working in QuickBooks for now, choose **File→Exit** from the menu bar.

Critical Thinking

In the course of working through the following Critical Thinking exercises, you will be utilizing various skills taught in this and previous lesson(s). Take your time and think carefully about the tasks presented to you. Turn back to the lesson content if you need assistance.

3.1 Sort Through the Stack

Before You Begin: Restore the Monkey Business Lesson 3 (Portable) file from your storage location. (Remember that the password is blank for Mary!)

You have been hired by Mary Minard to help her with her organization's books. She is the owner of Monkey Business, a nonprofit organization that provides low-income students with help in preparing for college placement exams and applying for scholarships. You have just sat down at her desk and found a pile of papers. It is your job to sort through the papers and make sense of what you find, entering information into QuickBooks whenever appropriate and answering any other questions in a word-processing document saved as **Critical Thinking 3-1**.

- Sticky note: New source for books—Enter Woods Publishing Company as a vendor: 921 Pamela Lake Drive, Salem, OR 97301; 503.555.2211; Terms—Net 30; Contact—Pam Woods.

- Bill: From Salem Power and Light, dated 7/3/2011, for $94.57, due 7/13/2011.

- Canceled check: Written to USPS for stamps on 7/2/2011 for $25.10, number 1003.

- Note: Would like to track employee anniversaries. How can I do that?

- Scribbled on a scrap of paper: I need a report that shows all of the bills that have been entered into QuickBooks.

- Packing slip and bill: Materials received for a FAFSA seminar; need to enter the bill for $124.32, payable to Chandler Distributors, dated 7/1/2011, terms Net 15. (Mary is not tracking inventory in QuickBooks!)

- Carbon copies of checks: Used to pay Salem Power and Light (#1004, 7/7/2011, for full amount) and Chandler Distributors (#1005, 7/7/2011, for full amount).

- Note: We have "customers" who are referred to us by the school district. Can we include them in the customer type list?

- Bill: From Willamette Cable for Internet and Phone service, dated 7/5/2011, for $112.65, due 7/15/2011.

- Printed email message from accountant: Please send a report that shows the amount owed to each vendor as of 7/10/2011.

- Bill: From Jones Brothers' Pizza for food provided at an event, dated 7/8/2011, payment due on receipt, for $67.21.

3.2 Tackle the Tasks

Now is your chance to work a little more with Chez Devereaux Salon and Spa and apply the skills that you have learned in this lesson to accomplish additional tasks. Restore the Critical Thinking 3.2 portable company file from your file storage location. Then, enter the following tasks.

Add a Vendor	Enter the following vendor: ■ Midwest Salon Unlimited 6439 Washington Square, Wausau, WI 54401 ■ Contact: Abby Gibbs, 715-555-9922 ■ Acct #: PR203X, Type: Suppliers, Terms: Net 15
Delete Profile List Entries	Delete Retail and Wholesale from the Customer Type List
Enter a Bill	Enter the following bill from Midwest Salon Unlimited: ■ Dated: 05/14/2011; Amt. $63.27 ■ Acct: 67400•Salon Supplies, Linens, Laundry
Pay Bills	■ Pay all bills due during the month of May. ■ Payment date: 05/18/2011; checks to be printed
Write and Print Checks	■ Write a check on 5/17/11 to Allen Brothers Grocery for $36.21 for Office Supplies, choose for it to be printed. ■ Print all checks waiting in the queue, first check #3002.
Display Reports	Display reports that will answer the following questions: ■ Which bills are due? ■ What is my company's current balance with each vendor? ■ What is the contact information and current balance for each vendor?

You may use the company file from this exercise for the Develop Your Skills exercise in Lesson 4 if you wish.

Working with Customers

LESSON OBJECTIVES

After studying this lesson, you will be able to:

- Use the Customer Center and Customers & Jobs List
- Create service and non-inventory items
- Deal with collecting and paying sales tax
- Create invoices and receive payment on them
- Enter sales receipts
- Work with customer-related and profit and loss reports

Let's face it. The best part of being in business is creating and developing relationships with customers. After all, who doesn't enjoy receiving payment for a job well done? Intuit describes a customer as "any person, business, or group that buys or pays for the services or products that your business or organization sells or provides." When working with QuickBooks, you can consider a customer anyone who pays you money. This simple definition will help you if you have a unique business, such as a not-for-profit organization that doesn't normally use the term "customer." The job feature is an optional aspect of QuickBooks, but the feature can be extremely helpful if you have more than one project for a customer. In this lesson, you will examine QuickBooks' lists, activities, and reports that allow you to effectively deal with customers.

Chez Devereaux Salon and Spa

Lisa has learned from her friend Adrianna that the next step she needs to complete is to set up her company to track customers and sales transactions. She will begin by working on her Customers & Jobs List, which is a part of the Customer Center. Once her customers have been entered, she will be able to create transactions for them. In order to create sales transactions such as invoices and sales receipts, though, she must first create items that will be used to direct income into the proper accounts behind the scenes. Finally, Lisa will create reports that will tell her about her customer-related transactions as well as a profit and loss report that will show the profitability of the business.

Lisa can access the Customers & Jobs List, and all of the transactions concerning a customer, from the Customer Center. The following illustration shows the Customer Center with Holly Rose selected.

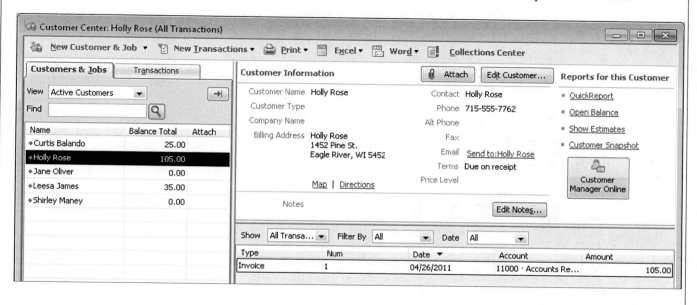

4.1 Working with the Customer Center

When opened, the Customer Center gives you a quick look at all of your customers. If you recall from the introduction, a customer is anyone who pays you money. This general definition is useful because it applies to all types of organizations, even those that do not have "customers" in the traditional sense, such as not-for-profits.

Remember that QuickBooks uses lists to organize your company's information. Lists allow you to store information that you can easily fill into forms by using drop-down arrows or by just starting to type the entry and letting QuickBooks fill in the rest. Lists comprise the database aspect of QuickBooks. As an option, the Customers & Jobs List can be exported to contact management software such as Microsoft Outlook.

The Customer Center window provides you with the following information:

- The name of each customer and any jobs that have been created
- The balance that each customer owes
- Information for the selected customer or job
- Transactions affecting the selected customer or job

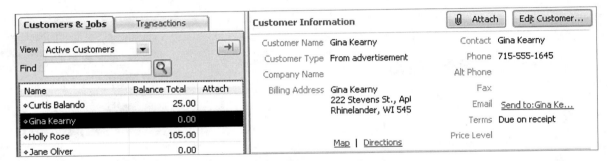

Notice that the Customer Information displayed to the right of the Customers & Jobs List in the Customer Center is that of the selected record.

The Customers & Jobs List tracks a lot of information for each customer and each job. This information is organized onto four tabs: Address Info, Additional Info, Payment Info, and Job Info. If you have jobs assigned to a customer, you will see only three tabs. You will manage the jobs in the separate job records. If you want to track information that does not already have a field, you can create Custom Fields to customize QuickBooks for your unique business, as you learned about in the previous lesson. Remember, the more information you enter for each customer, the more flexibility you will have later when you learn how to customize reports. When you utilize fields, you can sort, group, and filter your reports using those fields. You can access the Customers & Jobs List through the Customer Center.

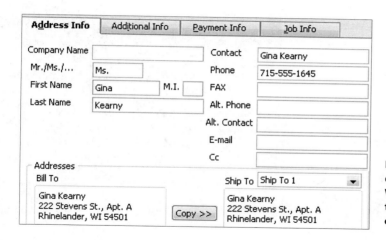

Note the four tabs on which you can enter information about a customer. When you create a job for a customer, that tab is eliminated, and the job will open in its own window.

Managing the Customers & Jobs List

The list management techniques that you learned about in Lesson 3, Working with Vendors are very similar for the Customers & Jobs List as well as the Employees List. The next three concepts will serve as a review of creating, editing, and deleting Customers & Jobs, Vendor, and Employees List entries.

Creating a New Customer

To enter customer transactions, you must first enter your customers into the Customers & Jobs List. Customers can be entered at any time and can even be entered "on the fly" into the customer field on forms such as Create Invoices and Enter Sales Receipts; you will then have to select Quick Add or Setup from the pop-up window. Once you have added a customer to the list, you can create individual jobs for that customer.

Editing an Existing Customer

Once you have created a customer, you can always go back and edit that customer through the Customer Center. The one item that cannot be edited after you have created and saved a new customer is the opening balance (it must be adjusted through the customer register).

Deleting a Customer

You can delete a customer or job from the Customers & Jobs List *as long as you have not used it in a transaction*.

QUICK REFERENCE	MANAGING THE CUSTOMER & JOB LIST
Task	**Procedure**
Edit an existing customer/job	■ Open the Customer Center, and then double-click the customer or job you wish to edit. ■ Make the change(s) in the field(s); click OK.
Add a new customer	■ Open the Customer Center. ■ Click the New Customer & Job button at the top of the window, and then choose New Customer from the menu. ■ Enter all of the customer's information; click OK.

Task	Procedure
Add a new job	■ Open the Customer Center, and then single-click the customer to whom you want to add a job.
	■ Click the New Customer & Job button at the top of the window, and then choose Add Job from the menu.
	■ Enter all of the information for the job; click OK.
Delete a customer/job	■ Open the Customer Center, and then single-click the customer/job you wish to delete.
	■ Choose Edit→Delete Customer:Job from the menu bar.
	■ Click OK to confirm the deletion.

DEVELOP YOUR SKILLS 4.1.1

Manage the Customers & Jobs List

In this exercise, you will track your customer information with the Customers & Jobs List.

Open a Portable Company File

You will start by opening a portable company file.

1. Launch **QuickBooks**.

    You may also continue to use the company file that you worked with in the Critical Thinking section of Lesson 3 (make sure you use only the file from the Critical Thinking 3.2, not Develop Your Skills). If you choose this option, open the company file in QuickBooks and then skip to step 5.

2. Choose **File→Open or Restore Company** from the menu bar.

3. **Open** the Chez Devereaux Salon and Spa Lesson 4 (Portable) file in your default storage location, placing your name as the first word in the filename (e.g., Lisa's Chez Devereaux Salon and Spa).

4. Click **OK** to close the QuickBooks Information window; click **No** in the Set Up External Accountant User window, if necessary.

FROM THE KEYBOARD

Ctrl+J to open the Customer Center

Edit an Existing Customer

The first step in performing any Customers & Jobs list management task is to open the Customer Center.

5. Open the Customer Center by clicking the **Customers** button located in the Customers area of the Home page.

6. **Single-click** to select **Leesa James** in the Customers & Jobs List.

    You must first select the customer you wish to edit.

7. Click the **Edit Customer** button in the Customer Information area of the Customer Center.

The Edit Customer window will open for Leesa James.

8. Correct the phone number to read **715-555-9831**.

9. Click **OK** to accept the change.

Add a New Customer

Now you will add a new customer to the Customers & Jobs List.

10. Click the **New Customers & Jobs** button and choose **New Customer** from the menu.

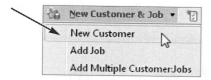

11. Follow these steps to fill in the information on the Address Info tab:

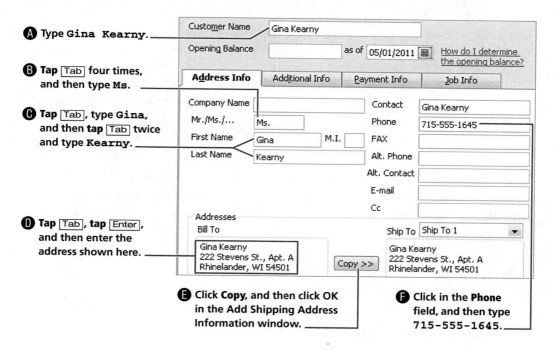

A Type **Gina Kearny**.

B Tap Tab four times, and then type **Ms.**

C Tap Tab, type **Gina**, and then **tap** Tab twice and type **Kearny**.

D Tap Tab, tap Enter, and then enter the address shown here.

E Click **Copy**, and then click OK in the Add Shipping Address Information window.

F Click in the **Phone** field, and then type **715-555-1645**.

12. Click the **Additional Info** tab; then, follow these steps to add information:

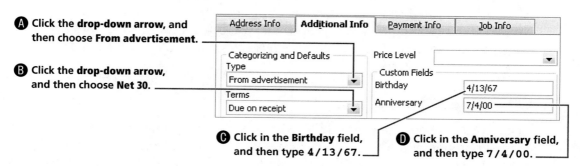

A Click the **drop-down arrow**, and then choose **From advertisement**.

B Click the **drop-down arrow**, and then choose **Net 30**.

C Click in the **Birthday** field, and then type **4/13/67**.

D Click in the **Anniversary** field, and then type **7/4/00**.

Notice that the custom fields are not formatted date fields, so the date you enter will appear as typed.

13. Click the **Payment Info** tab, and then type **A342** as the Account No.

14. Click **OK** to complete the new customer record.

15. Close the **Customer Center**, leaving the Home page open.

4.2 Dealing with Sales Tax in QuickBooks

QuickBooks makes it easy to charge and collect sales tax for items. You can also choose whether to charge tax for individual customers who resell merchandise to their customers and charge sales tax on the final sale rather than pay the tax to you. How you set up sales tax in QuickBooks depends entirely on which state(s) you conduct business in. There are some states that do not collect sales tax at all (yay, Oregon!), and there is variation among the others regarding what is taxed. Some states tax service that is performed, and others do not. Some tax grocery food items, and others do not. You must know the sales tax laws in your state before you set up sales tax for your company.

When dealing with sales tax, take some time to learn about how the sales tax laws are set up in your jurisdiction. How you display items on invoices, in both structure and whether items are stated separately or grouped together, can affect the amount of tax due on a transaction. Taking time up front can save you and your customers money in the long run.

Behind the scenes, the sales tax collected will be directed to a Sales Tax Liability account that QuickBooks automatically creates for you. The funds will be held there until you pay them to the appropriate governing authority.

Sales Tax Items and Groups

To include sales tax on a sales form, you must set up the tax as an item. An interesting situation arises, though, when you have to pay the tax collected to multiple tax agencies. QuickBooks helps you deal with this situation by allowing you to combine multiple sales tax items into a sales tax group. This is necessary, as you can apply only one sales tax item or group to a sales form. Before you can set up to collect sales tax, you must turn on the preference and create a sales tax item or group.

Default Tax Rate

Once you have created your sales tax item(s) and group(s), you should set up a default tax rate in your preferences. This rate will appear when you create a sales form for a customer for whom a tax rate is not specified. You should choose the tax rate that you use most of the time as the default; you can change it on a sale-by-sale basis.

Dealing with Multiple Sales Tax Rates

Some companies conduct business in multiple areas. As such, the company must set up different sales tax items and/or groups with the different rates. You can set one default tax rate for the company or default tax rates for each customer. Do this on the Additional Info tab of the New Customer and Edit Customer windows.

QUICK REFERENCE	SETTING UP THE SALES TAX FEATURE
Task	**Procedure**
Turn on the QuickBooks sales tax feature	■ Choose Edit→Preferences from the menu bar. ■ Click the Sales Tax category at the left of the window, and then click the Company Preferences tab. ■ Click in the circle to the left of Yes in the "Do you charge sales tax?" section of the window. ■ Select your most common sales tax item. If necessary, create the item using the steps detailed below. ■ Select when you owe sales tax and how often you must pay it. ■ Click OK to record the new preference.
Create a sales tax item	■ Open the Item List, click the Item menu button, and then click New. ■ Choose Sales Tax Item as the type of item (the sales tax preference must be set up first). ■ Type the name and description for the item. ■ Set the tax rate and agency to which you pay the tax; click OK.
Create a sales tax group	■ You must first set up the items that will be included in the group. ■ Open the Item List, click the Item menu button, and then click New. ■ Choose Sales Tax Group as the type. ■ Type the group name and description. ■ Choose each sales tax item that is to be included in the group; click OK.
Set your company's default tax rate	■ Choose Edit→Preferences from the menu bar. ■ Click the Sales Tax category at the left of the window, and then click the Company Preferences tab. ■ Choose your default tax rate from the Your most common sales tax item field drop-down button; click OK.
Set a customer's default tax rate	■ Open the Customer Center, and then double-click the customer whose default tax rate you wish to set. ■ Choose the Additional Info tab. ■ Choose the correct tax rate from the Tax Item field drop-down arrow; click OK.

Set Up QuickBooks to Collect Sales Tax

You will now help Lisa set up QuickBooks to collect sales tax by turning on the preference and creating sales tax items and a sales tax group.

Turn On the Sales Tax Preference and Create a Sales Tax Item

Before a sales tax item can be set up, you must turn on the preference in QuickBooks.

1. Choose **Edit→Preferences** from the menu bar.

2. Follow these steps to turn on the sales tax preference:

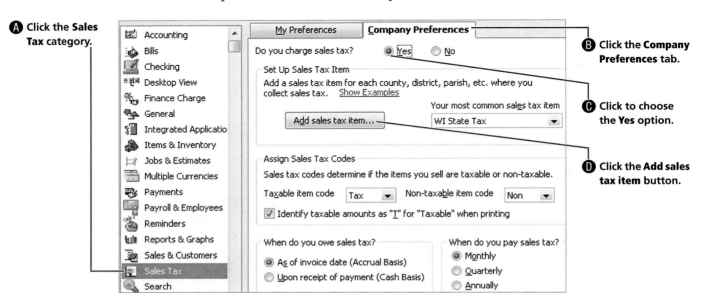

Ⓐ Click the **Sales Tax category.**

Ⓑ Click the **Company Preferences tab.**

Ⓒ Click to choose the **Yes** option.

Ⓓ Click the **Add sales tax item** button.

You will now have a New Item window open so you can create your first sales tax item.

 In the next step, you will Quick Add Oneida County Treasurer as a vendor for the tax item. It is important to have all of the vendor's information entered in the Vendor List. In your own company file, make sure to either set up your tax agency vendors at this point or return to the Vendor Center to add the information later in the Edit Vendor window.

3. Follow these steps to add an additional sales tax item:

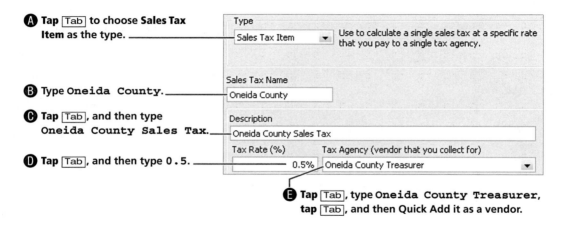

Ⓐ Tap Tab to choose **Sales Tax Item** as the type.

Ⓑ Type **Oneida County.**

Ⓒ Tap Tab, and then type **Oneida County Sales Tax.**

Ⓓ Tap Tab, and then type **0.5.**

Ⓔ Tap Tab, type **Oneida County Treasurer,** tap Tab, and then Quick Add it as a vendor.

4. Click **OK**.

5. Click **Add** in the Check Spelling on Form window, if necessary, but only after you have ensured that "Oneida" is spelled correctly.

 Realize that the spell check feature can check your entries only against the dictionary that is in QuickBooks. So, you may have spelled something correctly, but QuickBooks won't recognize it as correct. Adding "Oneida" in the step above put the word in the QuickBooks dictionary. In the future, that word will not trigger the spell check feature.

Create a Sales Tax Group

Now that you have created the two items that comprise the total amount of the sales tax in Rhinelander, WI, you can create a sales tax group that includes both of them. The Preferences window should still be open with the Company Preferences tab of the Sales Tax category displayed.

6. Click the **Add** sales tax item button again.

7. Follow these steps to create a new sales tax group:

A Click **Sales Tax Group** from the Type list.

B Tap `Tab`, and then type `Oneida ST Group`.

C Tap `Tab`, and then type `Total Sales Tax for Oneida County`.

D Tap `Tab`, and then type `o` so QuickBooks will fill in "Oneida County" as the first Tax Item.

E Tap `Tab`, type `w`, and then tap `Tab` again.

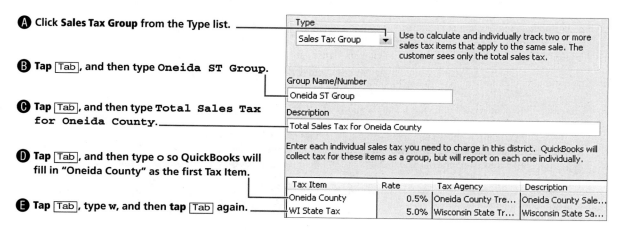

As you choose the items, QuickBooks will fill in all information for each tax item and calculate the group rate (5.5%) for you.

8. Click **OK** to both add the new Sales Tax Group and close the **New Item** window.

Set Oneida ST Group as the Default Tax Rate

Remember that when you turned on the sales tax preference, WI State Tax showed up as the default for your company file. Now you will set your group tax rate to be your default.

9. Click the **drop-down arrow**, and then choose **Oneida ST Group** for the Your most common sales tax item field.

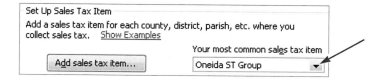

10. Click **OK** to add the new preference.
QuickBooks prompts you with update options.

11. Click **OK** in the Updating Sales Tax window; then, click **OK** to acknowledge the closing of all open windows.
You will leave the defaults chosen as to when you owe sales tax and how often you pay it. When working with your own company, make sure you choose the correct options for your company in these sections.

4.3 Understanding and Creating Items

Before you can create an invoice, you must create items to be included on the invoice. You have already created items for sales tax, so you will now create items for service and non-inventory items. An item is defined in QuickBooks as something that a company buys, sells, or resells in the course of business.

When you create a new item, you need to provide QuickBooks with very important information. When an item is sold, it directs the sales to the proper income account based on the information you entered when you created the item. The Item List will be studied in more depth in *QuickBooks Pro 2011: Level 2,* when you begin to work with inventory. In this lesson, you will access the Item List through the Home page.

This column shows the name of the items. This is what you will enter into a form to choose the item.

There is a search feature displayed at the top of the Item List window. This can come in handy if you have a large number of items through which you may need to look to find a specific item.

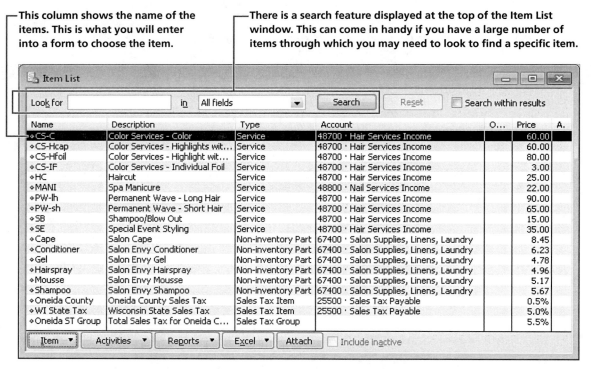

The Item List displays all of the items that you have available to include on sales forms.

Service Items

Service items are used in QuickBooks to track services that you both sell to others and purchase from them. They can be used to track time that employees spend on a certain customer's project and then easily passed on to a customer using the QuickBooks time-tracking feature as well. This use of service items will be covered in *QuickBooks Pro 2011: Level 2*.

Non-Inventory Items

Non-inventory part items are for things that a business buys but doesn't stock as inventory. You can use purchase orders to obtain non-inventory items if you wish to track items that are used in your business but not resold to customers, such as brushes, shampoo, and hairspray. You will learn more about purchase orders in *QuickBooks Pro 2011: Level 2*. In order to track both purchase and sales information for an item, you need to identify that the item is "used in assemblies or is purchased for a specific customer:job" in the New or Edit Item window.

This list displays the types of items that can be created. Inventory Part is not shown at this time because this feature is not yet turned on.

If you check this box, you can indicate both purchase and sales information for the item. This option is available for both non-inventory and service items.

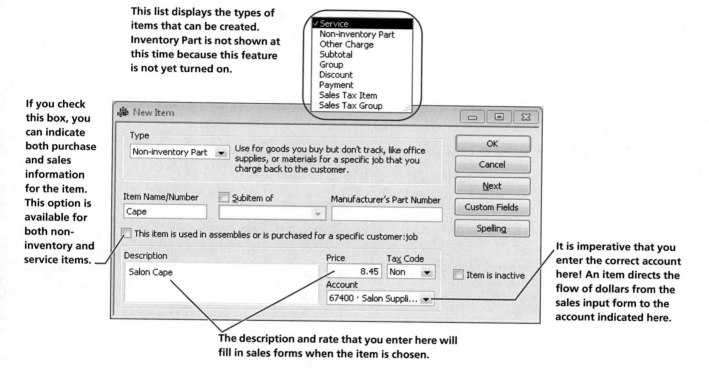

It is imperative that you enter the correct account here! An item directs the flow of dollars from the sales input form to the account indicated here.

The description and rate that you enter here will fill in sales forms when the item is chosen.

When you enter an item on a QuickBooks form, you can override the price that you have recorded in the Item List. If you don't have standard pricing and find that you enter specialized pricing more than you use a default price, you may wish to leave the Price field as zero in the Item List and fill it in on each form created.

Task	Procedure
Create a new item	▪ Open the Item List.
	▪ Click the item menu button, choose New, and then choose the type of item you wish to create.
	▪ Enter an item name and description.
	▪ Enter the rate or price for the item.
	▪ Select the account (income for a service item, expense, or cost of goods sold for a non-inventory item), to which you want the purchase of the item directed.

DEVELOP YOUR SKILLS 4.3.1

Create Items

In this exercise, you will create both a service and a non-inventory item.

Create a Service Item

1. Click the **Home** button on the icon bar.

2. Click the **Items & Services** task icon in the Company area of the Home page.

3. Click the **Item** menu button and choose **New** from the menu.

4. **Tap** Tab and the default service item type, Service, is chosen automatically.

5. Follow these steps to create a new service item:

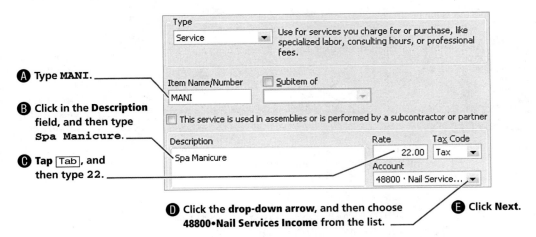

Ⓐ Type **MANI**.

Ⓑ Click in the **Description** field, and then type **Spa Manicure**.

Ⓒ Tap Tab, and then type **22**.

Ⓓ Click the **drop-down arrow**, and then choose **48800•Nail Services Income** from the list.

Ⓔ Click **Next**.

The new item will be added to the Item List and the New Item window will remain open so you can create another item. Notice the Tax Code field that indicates that this item is taxable.

Set Up a Non-Inventory Item

6. Follow these steps to create a new non-inventory part:

Ⓐ Click the **drop-down arrow**, and then choose **Non-inventory Part.**

Ⓑ Tap `Tab`, and then type **Cape.**

Ⓒ Click in the **Description** field, and then type **Salon Cape.**

Ⓓ Tap `Tab`, and then type **8.45.**

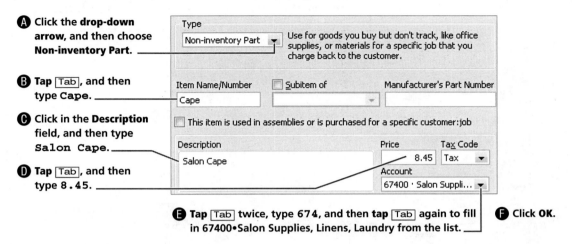

Ⓔ Tap `Tab` twice, type **674**, and then tap `Tab` again to fill in 67400•Salon Supplies, Linens, Laundry from the list.

Ⓕ Click **OK.**

7. Close the **Item** window.

4.4 Creating Invoices

Once you have set up your initial Customers & Jobs List, you can begin to enter sales transactions. In this section, you will learn to create invoices and use accounts receivable, which is the account debited when invoices are created. When you create an invoice, you *must* specify a customer because accounts receivable (along with the customer's individual sub-register) will be debited by the transaction.

After you select your customer from the drop-down list at the top of the form, all of the relevant information you entered in that customer's record will fill into the appropriate fields on the Create Invoices window. If you wish to create an invoice for a new customer not yet entered into the Customers & Jobs List, QuickBooks will allow you to create the new list record "on the fly," just as you did for vendors.

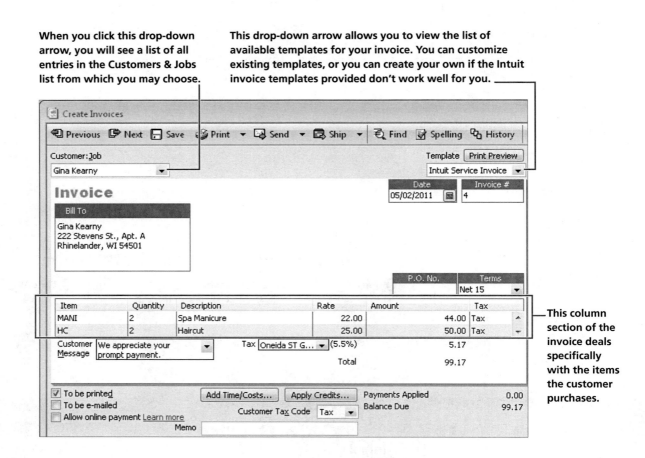

When you click this drop-down arrow, you will see a list of all entries in the Customers & Jobs list from which you may choose.

This drop-down arrow allows you to view the list of available templates for your invoice. You can customize existing templates, or you can create your own if the Intuit invoice templates provided don't work well for you.

This column section of the invoice deals specifically with the items the customer purchases.

When you created your customer records, you entered a lot of information about each customer that will automatically fill into invoices when the customer is chosen. You have the option of changing that information when you create an invoice, though. If you change a customer's information in the Create Invoices window, QuickBooks will ask if you want to make the change permanent before recording the transaction.

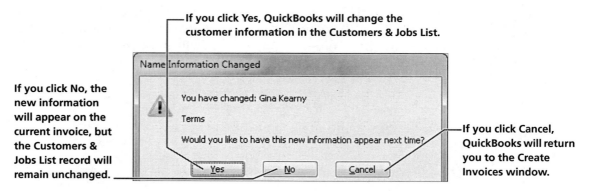

If you click Yes, QuickBooks will change the customer information in the Customers & Jobs List.

If you click No, the new information will appear on the current invoice, but the Customers & Jobs List record will remain unchanged.

If you click Cancel, QuickBooks will return you to the Create Invoices window.

Entering Customers Not Already on the Customers & Jobs List

You can enter customers "on the fly" in sales forms just as you did with vendors in the last lesson by simply typing them into the Customer:Job field. Once you enter the customer that is not in the Customers & Jobs List, you will have an option to Quick Add or Setup the new customer before completing the rest of the form.

Form Templates

When you first install QuickBooks, Intuit provides you with various templates, such as the Intuit Service Invoice, Intuit Product Invoice, Intuit Professional Invoice, and Intuit Packing Slip. You can continue to use these invoices as they are, create custom invoices to meet your specific needs, or download templates from the QuickBooks website. In this section, you will work with one of the default invoice forms—the Intuit Service Invoice. The creation and customization of form templates will be covered in *QuickBooks Pro 2011: Level 2*.

BEHIND THE SCENES

When creating invoices, QuickBooks takes care of all of the accounting for you. Following is an illustration of the accounting that goes on behind the scenes for the second invoice you will create in the following exercise.

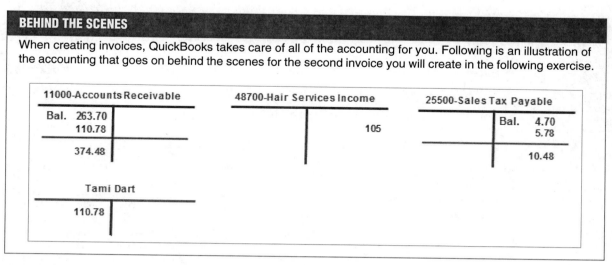

QUICK REFERENCE | CREATING INVOICES

Task	Procedure
Create an invoice	■ Open the Create Invoices window.
	■ Choose an existing customer or type a new customer.
	■ Choose the correct date and terms.
	■ Fill in the item(s) for which you wish to bill your customer, including the correct quantity for each item.
	■ Choose a customer message, if desired, and then click Save & Close or Save & New.

DEVELOP YOUR SKILLS 4.4.1

Create Invoices

In this exercise, you will create invoices for customers.

Create an Invoice for an Existing Customer

FROM THE KEYBOARD

Ctrl+I to open the Create Invoices window

Gina Kearny has just come in with her daughter for manicures and haircuts. You have agreed to grant her terms of "Net 15," which means that her bill will be due in 15 days.

1. Click the **Create Invoices** task icon in the Customers area of the Home page.

2. Click the **No Thanks** button in the Customize Your QuickBooks Forms window, if necessary.

3. Click the **Customer:Job** field drop-down arrow at the top of the window, and then choose **Gina Kearny** from the Customers & Jobs List.

Notice that the customer's address and terms fill in for you from the underlying list.

4. Tap ⟨Tab⟩ three times, type **050211**, and then **tap** ⟨Tab⟩.
Notice that QuickBooks fills in number 4 for the invoice (there are already three existing invoices for the company). You can either use the auto numbering feature or type your own invoice number.

5. Follow these steps to complete the invoice:

Ⓐ Click the **drop-down arrow**, and then choose **Net 15.**

Ⓑ Tap ⟨Tab⟩, type **m**, tap ⟨Tab⟩, and then type **2.**

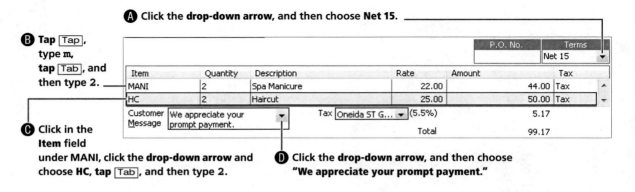

Ⓒ Click in the **Item** field under MANI, click the **drop-down arrow** and choose **HC**, tap ⟨Tab⟩, and then type **2.**

Ⓓ Click the **drop-down arrow**, and then choose **"We appreciate your prompt payment."**

Once you select the item, the description, rate, and amount information fill in for you from the Item List. QuickBooks automatically calculates the total amount by multiplying the quantity by the rate. If you need to adjust the rate, you can replace the rate that filled in from the Item List, and QuickBooks will recalculate the amount once you move your insertion point to another field on the invoice form.

6. Click the **Save & New** button; then, click **No** in the Name Information Changed window.
A Name Information Changed window appeared since you changed the terms for the customer.

Create an Invoice for a New Customer

A new customer, Tami Dart, has stopped by the salon. You will add her as a new customer "on the fly" while creating the invoice for her. Your insertion point should be in the Customer:Job field at the top of a new invoice. If this is not the case, choose Customers→Create Invoices from the menu bar.

7. Type **Tami Dart**, and then **tap** ⟨Tab⟩.
The Customer:Job Not Found window will be displayed.

8. Click **Quick Add** in the Customer:Job list window, and then **tap** ⟨Tab⟩ three times to go to the **Date** field.

9. Tap ⊞ until the date reads **05/04/2011**.

10. Follow these steps to complete the invoice:

FROM THE KEYBOARD

⊞ to increase the date by one day at a time

⊟ to decrease the date by one day at a time

⊺ in a Date field to enter today's date

A Click the drop-down arrow and choose Net 15.

B Click in the Item column, and then type **hc** to choose it from the list.

		P.O. No.	Terms
			Net 15

Item	Quantity	Description	Rate	Amount	Tax
HC		Haircut	25.00	25.00	Tax
CS-Hfoil		Color Services - Highlight with Foils	80.00	80.00	Tax

Customer Message: It's been a pleasure working with you!

Tax: Oneida ST G... (5.5%) 5.78

Total 110.78

C Click below HC, and then click the drop-down arrow and choose CS-Hfoil from the list.

D Tap Alt+m, and then type **i**.

If the quantity is one item, you do not have to enter anything in the Quantity field. It is up to you if you choose to do so.

FROM THE KEYBOARD

Alt+m to move to the Customer Message field

When you see a field name that has an underlined letter, you can tap the Alt key as well as the underlined letter to move to that field quickly.

11. Click **Save & Close**; then, click **Yes** in the Name Information Changed window.

4.5 Receiving Payments

Once you have created invoices, you need to be able to accept the payments on them from your customers. In QuickBooks, you will use the Receive Payments window to credit Accounts Receivable and the appropriate customer sub-register. The other half of the equation (the account that will be debited) depends on how you treat the payments you receive.

It is very important to use the Receive Payments window to enter payments received from invoiced customers. If you don't, the invoices will remain open, and your income and the amounts in accounts receivable will be overstated.

FLASHBACK TO GAAP: MATCHING

Remember that expenses need to be matched with revenues.

Accept Payment Options

There is a Payment Toolbar that fills the left side of the Receive Payments and Enter Sales Receipts windows. It opens by default and is designed to provide options to assist you with a variety of payment situations.

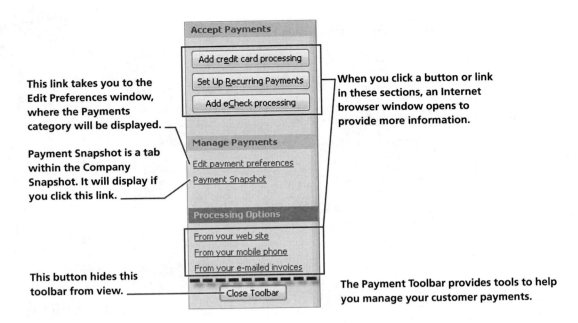

This link takes you to the Edit Preferences window, where the Payments category will be displayed.

Payment Snapshot is a tab within the Company Snapshot. It will display if you click this link.

This button hides this toolbar from view.

When you click a button or link in these sections, an Internet browser window opens to provide more information.

The Payment Toolbar provides tools to help you manage your customer payments.

The Undeposited Funds Account

If you typically collect payments from more than one source before making a deposit, you will want to choose to group all payments in QuickBooks using the Undeposited Funds account. QuickBooks automatically creates this Other Current Asset account for you.

The default setting is for all payment receipts and cash sales to be placed in the Undeposited Funds account. You can change this preference in the Payments category of the Edit Preferences window.

Once you are ready to make a deposit to the bank, you will use the Make Deposit window, where you can select the payments in the Undeposited Funds account that you wish to deposit. You will learn about making deposits in QuickBooks in the next lesson.

BEHIND THE SCENES

Let's look at accounting scenarios that result when you receive payments.

11000-Accounts Receivable		12000-Undeposited Funds	
Bal. 374.48	99.17	99.17	
275.31			

Using the Undeposited Funds account when receiving a customer payment

11000-Accounts Receivable		10000-Checking	
Bal. 374.48	99.17	99.17	
275.31			

Depositing a customer payment directly into a bank account

DEVELOP YOUR SKILLS 4.5.1

Receive Payments

In this exercise, you will deal with payments received from invoiced customers.

Receive a Payment

You have just received a payment from Gina Kearny.

1. Click the **Receive Payments** task icon in the Customers area of the Home page.
   The Receive Payments window opens with the insertion point in the Received From field.

2. Follow these steps to enter a customer payment:

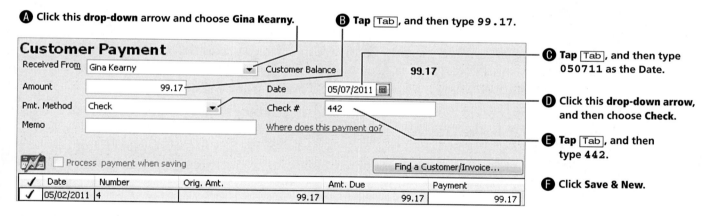

Ⓐ Click this **drop-down** arrow and choose **Gina Kearny.**

Ⓑ Tap [Tab], and then type 99.17.

Ⓒ Tap [Tab], and then type 050711 as the Date.

Ⓓ Click this **drop-down arrow,** and then choose **Check.**

Ⓔ Tap [Tab], and then type 442.

Ⓕ Click Save & New.

Notice that when you typed the amount, QuickBooks automatically applied it to the invoice listed. If you had multiple invoices displayed, QuickBooks would first apply the payment to the invoice that was for the exact amount. If no invoices matched the amount, it would be applied to invoice(s) beginning with the oldest one.

Receive a Partial Payment

Holly Rose just sent in $50 to apply to her outstanding invoice. You will receive this payment.

3. Type **h**, and then **tap** [Tab].

4. Follow these steps to complete the payment receipt:

Ⓐ Type 50 in the Amount field.

Ⓑ Tap [Tab], and then tap [+] to change the date to 5/9/11.

Ⓒ Tap [Tab] twice, and then type 892.

QuickBooks applies the payment to the outstanding invoice. The next time you select Holly Rose as the customer in the Receive Payments window, QuickBooks will show that there is a balance due of $60.78. Notice that QuickBooks gives you an option as to how to deal with underpayments on invoices while you're still in the Received Payments window.

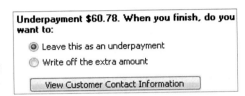

5. Click **Save & Close** once you have ensured that you have entered all information correctly.

4.6 Entering Sales Receipts

As discussed earlier, you can use either of two forms to enter sales transactions. You have already learned how to create invoices and about the effect that they have behind the scenes. Now you will learn how to enter cash sales when payment is received up front.

A company does not have to choose one method of recording sales transactions and stick with it. Both forms can be used for the same company, depending on the situation at hand. When entering cash sales, you do not have to enter a customer (as accounts receivable is not affected) although you may want to enter customers to produce more meaningful sales reports. You have the option of adding a customer "on the fly" in the Enter Sales Receipts window just as you do when creating invoices.

As with the Receive Payments window, you can set a preference in order to be able to choose whether to group your payment with other funds waiting to be deposited or directly deposit it in the bank. The default option is to place all payments in the Undeposited Funds account. If you change the preference, you will need to choose into which account to deposit each payment.

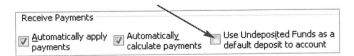

When you deselect the "Use Undeposited Funds as a default deposit to account" preference, a Deposit To field will appear on the Create Sales Receipts and Receive Payments windows so you may choose into which asset account you wish the payment to go, as displayed on the next page.

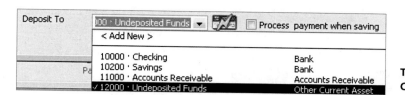

The Deposit To field on the Create Sales Receipts window

You should notice how the Enter Sales Receipt form differs from the Create Invoices form and is essentially a combination of the Create Invoices and Receive Payments windows.

"JIT" Transaction History

A new feature in QuickBooks 2011 is a summary of customer or vendor information in the transaction windows just when you need it (or "just in time"). This will allow you to see a recent transaction history when you are entering a new transaction, thus saving you from having to look it up.

Tami Dart	
	Edit Customer
Summary	
Open balance	110.25
Active estimates	0
Sales Orders to be invoiced	0
Recent Transactions	QuickReport
05/04/11 Invoice	110.25
Notes	Edit

The transaction history for Tami Dart will appear on the right side of the Enter Sales Receipts window once you have selected her as the customer.

The summary transaction history is a new feature in QuickBooks 2011. It will be displayed in a variety of windows to aid you in making business decisions as you enter information in QuickBooks.

BEHIND THE SCENES

The behind the scenes accounting that occurs when you enter cash sales is a hybrid of the two previous transactions (Creating Invoices and Receiving Payments) with the elimination of the middleman—Accounts Receivable.

10000-Checking, or 12000-Undeposited Funds	48700-Hair Services Income	25500-Sales Tax Payable
36.93	35.00	1.93

QUICK REFERENCE   ENTERING CASH SALES

Task	Procedure
Enter a cash sale	■ Open the Enter Sales Receipts window and choose a customer, if desired.
	■ Enter the date of the transaction, payment method, and reference/check number.
	■ Enter the items and quantity sold.
	■ Select a message for the customer, if desired.
	■ Click Save & Close or Save & New, depending on whether you wish to enter another cash sale.

Enter Cash Sales

In this exercise, you will receive payment at the time of the sale.

Record a Cash Sale for a Specific Customer

1. Click the **Create Sales Receipts** task icon in the Customers area of the Home page.
   The Enter Sales Receipts window opens with the insertion point in the Customer:Job field.

2. Type **t** to bring up Tami Dart, and then **tap** Tab three times.

3. Follow these steps to complete the cash sale:

Ⓐ Use the ⊞ key to change the date to **5/14/11.**   **Ⓑ** Tap Tab three times, and then type **1539.**

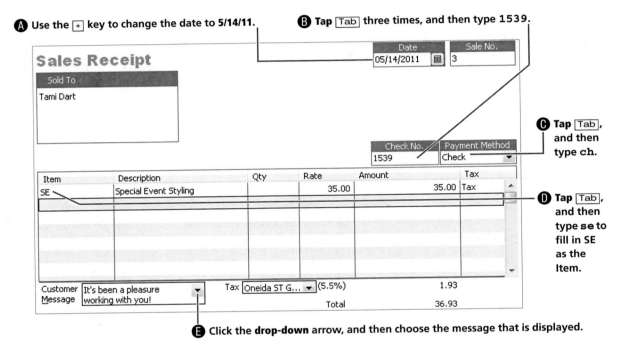

Ⓒ Tap Tab, and then type **ch.**

Ⓓ Tap Tab, and then type **se** to fill in SE as the Item.

Ⓔ Click the **drop-down** arrow, and then choose the message that is displayed.

4. Click **Save & New.**
   Your insertion point should be in the Customer:Job field of a new Enter Sales Receipt window.

Record a Sales Receipt Without a Specified Customer

Since Accounts Receivable is not affected when you enter a cash sale, you can create a sales receipt without choosing a customer. This may come in handy if you sell something to someone just once and don't need that customer listed in your Customers & Jobs List. In this exercise, Lisa worked with another stylist to style hair for a wedding party.

5. Tap Tab three times to move to the date field.

6. Follow these steps to complete the sales receipt:

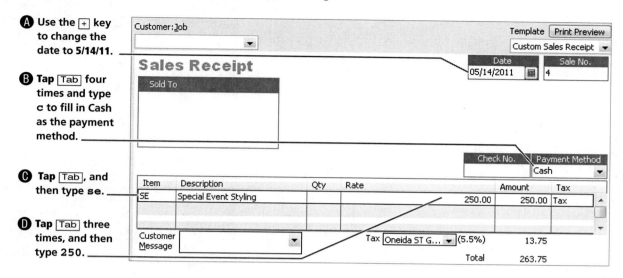

Ⓐ Use the ⊞ key to change the date to **5/14/11**.

Ⓑ Tap [Tab] four times and type **c** to fill in Cash as the payment method.

Ⓒ Tap [Tab], and then type **se**.

Ⓓ Tap [Tab] three times, and then type **250**.

7. Click **Save & Close.**

This transaction will debit Undeposited Funds and credit Hair Services Income, but there will be no customer tracked. The purpose of selecting a customer for a sales receipt is to ensure that you can produce meaningful customer reports, such as Sales by Customer Summary, if they are important to your business.

4.7 Paying Sales Tax

You have been collecting sales tax for your sales. Now it is time to learn how to pay the collected tax to the appropriate tax agencies.

Sales Tax Payable

As you have seen, when you bill a customer and collect sales tax, QuickBooks holds the funds in a current liability account. These taxes are never actually the property of your business (an asset), so you have been using a liabilities payable account as a place to "store" the taxes until it is time to remit them.

When you are ready to pay your sales tax, it is *imperative* that you do so through the Pay Sales Tax window. This is to ensure that the proper liability account is affected behind the scenes when the payment is processed.

When you are ready to pay sales tax, you *must* use the proper procedure, or you will not "empty" the Sales Tax Payable account behind the scenes.

The Sales Tax Liability Report

You can choose to run a sales tax liability report to see what funds you are holding in your sales tax payable account. This report will give you the values you need to file your sales tax return: total sales, taxable sales, nontaxable sales, and the amount of tax collected.

The Manage Sales Tax Window

The Manage Sales Tax window helps you manage all of your sales tax activities and reports easily by providing links to all of the tasks you will be performing when working with sales tax, from setting it up to paying it.

Dealing with Adjustments in Sales Tax

There are many situations that could result in an incorrect amount in the Pay Sales Tax window or on the sales tax liability report. You may have charged a customer a tax rate for the wrong jurisdiction or tax may have been charged for a nontaxable item. There could also be rounding errors, penalties, or credits/discounts that you need to take into account.

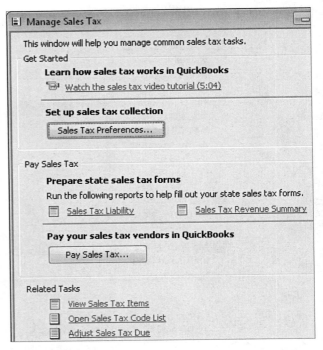

The Manage Sales Tax window helps you to deal with all of the QuickBooks preferences, activities, and reports related to sales tax.

You can make an adjustment to the tax owed through the Pay Sales Tax window or by choosing Adjust Sales Tax Due from the Vendors menu. Make sure that you don't use Sales Tax Payable as the "pay from account." Instead, you should use the following types of accounts.

- **For a rounding error:** You can set up a special account or use Miscellaneous Expense. Some businesses opt to create a special income account for a negative error or a special expense account for a positive error.
- **For a credit or to apply a discount:** Use an income account such as Other Income.
- **For interest due, fines, or penalties:** Use an expense account such as Interest Expense or Non-deductible Penalties.

If you make an adjustment to the sales tax liability account, you will need to choose the adjustment the next time you pay sales tax in order to get the correct amount to pay.

Changing a Tax Jurisdiction

In the situation where a customer was charged sales tax for the wrong jurisdiction, you need to go back to the original transaction and choose the correct sales tax item or group. If you charged tax on a nontaxable item (or vice versa), you will need to adjust the invoice or sales receipt where the sale was made. This may require you to issue a credit to the customer if they overpaid or reissue the invoice/receipt (or a statement) if the customer underpaid.

When you pay sales tax, behind the scenes you will see the funds leave the Sales Tax Payable account.

25500-Sales Tax Payable		10000-Checking	
62.41			62.41

QUICK REFERENCE	DEALING WITH SALES TAX
Task	**Procedure**
Pay sales tax	▪ Choose Vendors→Sales Tax→Pay Sales Tax.
	▪ Choose the bank account from which you will be paying the taxes.
	▪ Enter the date of the check and the date through which you wish to show sales taxes.
	▪ Choose which taxes to pay by clicking in the Pay column; click OK.
Run a sales tax liability report	▪ Choose Reports→Vendors & Payables→Sales Tax Liability from the menu bar.
	▪ Set the correct date range for the report.
Adjust the amount of sales tax owed	▪ Choose Vendors→Sales Tax→Adjust Sales Tax Due from the menu bar.
	▪ Enter the date, vendor, account, amount, and memo.
	▪ Click OK.

DEVELOP YOUR SKILLS 4.7.1

Pay Sales Tax

In this exercise, you will help Lisa pay the sales tax that she has collected to the appropriate tax agencies.

Enter a Sales Tax Penalty

Lisa just received a notice from the State of Wisconsin stating that the company has incurred a $30 penalty. In this exercise, you will help her enter the required transaction.

1. Click the **Manage Sales Tax** task icon in the Vendors area of the Home page.
   QuickBooks displays the Manage Sales Tax window.

2. Click the **Adjust Sales Tax Due** link at the bottom of the window.

3. Follow these steps to complete the adjustment:

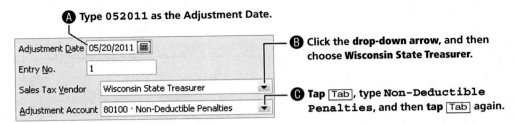

Ⓐ Type **052011** as the Adjustment Date.

Ⓑ Click the **drop-down arrow**, and then choose **Wisconsin State Treasurer**.

Ⓒ Tap ⎡Tab⎤, type `Non-Deductible Penalties`, and then tap ⎡Tab⎤ again.

QuickBooks displays a prompt that asks you to set up a new account.

4. Click the **Set Up** button; then, follow these steps to set up the account and finish the tax adjustment transaction:

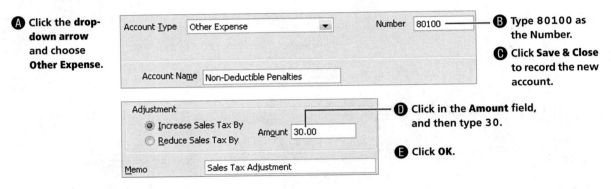

Ⓐ Click the **drop-down arrow** and choose **Other Expense**.

Ⓑ Type **80100** as the Number.

Ⓒ Click **Save & Close** to record the new account.

Ⓓ Click in the **Amount** field, and then type **30**.

Ⓔ Click **OK**.

You use Other Expense for this penalty as it was not incurred as a result of the regular course of business.

Determine How Much You Owe

The next step is to run a report to determine how much sales tax you owe and to whom you owe it.

5. Click the **Sales Tax Liability** link in the Manage Sales Tax window.

6. Tap ⎡Tab⎤ and type **050111**; then, **tap** ⎡Tab⎤ again, and then type **053111** to set the date range.

7. Click the **Refresh** button on the report toolbar.
Take a look at the information this report contains. The information you need to pay and file your taxes is in the last column, Sales Tax Payable as of May 31, 11. Notice that the amount owed to the Wisconsin State Treasurer has increased by the amount of the penalty.

8. Close the **Sales Tax Liability** report, choosing **No** when QuickBooks asks if you want to memorize the report.

Pay the Sales Tax

From the report you just ran, you know that Lisa currently owes $2.43 to Oneida County and $62.48 to the State of Wisconsin.

9. Click the **Pay Sales Tax** button in the Manage Sales Tax window.

10. Ensure that **10000•Checking** is the Pay From Account; then, follow these steps to pay the taxes due:

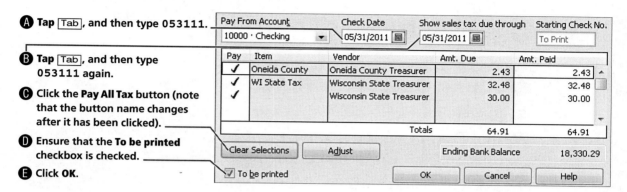

Ⓐ Tap Tab, and then type **053111**.

Ⓑ Tap Tab, and then type **053111** again.

Ⓒ Click the **Pay All Tax** button (note that the button name changes after it has been clicked).

Ⓓ Ensure that the **To be printed** checkbox is checked.

Ⓔ Click **OK**.

Pay From Account		Check Date	Show sales tax due through	Starting Check No.
10000 · Checking		05/31/2011	05/31/2011	To Print

Pay	Item	Vendor	Amt. Due	Amt. Paid
✓	Oneida County	Oneida County Treasurer	2.43	2.43
✓	WI State Tax	Wisconsin State Treasurer	32.48	32.48
✓		Wisconsin State Treasurer	30.00	30.00
		Totals	64.91	64.91

Clear Selections   Adjust   Ending Bank Balance   18,330.29

☑ To be printed   OK   Cancel   Help

Pay your sales tax vendors in QuickBooks
Pay Sales Tax...

The liability check has now been entered into the queue of checks to be printed.

11. Close the **Manage Sales Tax** window.

4.8 Working with Customer-Related and P&L Reports

You learned in the last two lessons that there are many preset reports you can run to display vendor transactions and list information. The same is true for customer- and company-related transactions.

Now that you have recorded both income and expenses for May, you will be able to run a meaningful profit and loss (P&L) report. It is important to make sure all income and expense transactions are entered so that income is matched to expenses for the period you are reporting. A P&L is a financial report that can be found in the Company & Financial category of the Report Center window. The P&L report will reflect all transactions that have affected income and expense accounts.

FLASHBACK TO GAAP: TIME PERIOD

Remember that it is implied that the activities of the business can be divided into time periods.

Task	Procedure
Produce a customer-related report using the Report Center	■ Choose Reports→Report Center from the menu bar. ■ Choose Customers & Receivables as the report category. ■ Click on the report you wish to produce in the main section of the Report Center. ■ Click the Display report button.
Produce a profit & loss report	■ Choose Reports→Company & Financial→Profit & Loss Standard from the menu bar.

DEVELOP YOUR SKILLS 4.8.1

Produce Customer-Related and P&L Reports

In this exercise, you will help Lisa create customer and profit and loss reports.

Run an Open Invoices Report

QuickBooks provides a report for you that displays all unpaid invoices. You will produce this for Lisa now.

1. Click the **Report Center** button on the icon bar.

2. Follow these steps to create an Open Invoices report:

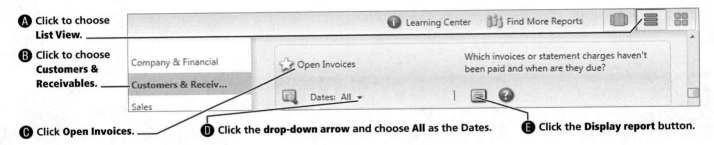

Ⓐ Click to choose List View.

Ⓑ Click to choose Customers & Receivables.

Ⓒ Click Open Invoices.

Ⓓ Click the **drop-down arrow** and choose **All** as the Dates.

Ⓔ Click the **Display report** button.

QuickBooks will display the Open Invoices report, which shows all unpaid invoices.

3. Close the **Open Invoices** report and the Report Center.

Create a Profit and Loss Report

Lisa would now like to see if the company had a net income or loss for May based on the transactions entered.

4. Choose **Reports→Company & Financial→Profit & Loss Standard** from the menu bar.
Remember that you can display all of the reports available through the Report Center via the menu bar as well.

5. Follow these steps to set the correct date range:

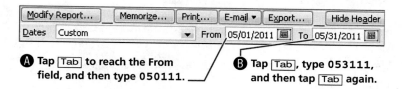

A Tap [Tab] to reach the From field, and then type **050111**.

B Tap [Tab], type **053111**, and then tap [Tab] again.

You will see a report that shows your total income and expenses for the time period along with the resulting net income (or loss). The income portion of your report should match the illustration at right. Notice that the date range is set to Custom on the toolbar. QuickBooks gives you the option to set the exact date range you desire in your reports.

6. Close the **Profit & Loss** report, choosing not to memorize the report.

7. Choose the appropriate option for your situation:

- If you are continuing on to the next lesson or to the end-of-lesson exercises, leave QuickBooks open and move on to the next exercise.

- If you are finished working in QuickBooks for now, choose **File→Exit** from the menu bar.

Chez Devereaux Salon and Spa
Profit & Loss
May 2011

	◇ May 11 ◇
Ordinary Income/Expense	
Income	
48700 · Hair Services Income	▶ 440.00 ◀
48800 · Nail Services Income	44.00
Total Income	484.00
Gross Profit	484.00

4.9 Concepts Review

Concepts Review labyrinthelab.com/qb11_level01

To check your knowledge of the key concepts introduced in this lesson, complete the Concepts Review quiz by going to the URL listed above.

Reinforce Your Skills

Before you begin the Reinforce Your Skills exercises, complete one of these options:

■ *Open the file [Your name]'s Tea Shoppe at the Lake from your file storage location that you used for Lesson 3.*

■ *Restore the Lesson 4 Tea Shoppe at the Lake file from your file storage location. If you need to review how to restore a portable company file, take a peek at Develop Your Skills 3.1.1. Make sure to place your name as the first word in the company filename (e.g., Susie's Tea Shoppe at the Lake).*

REINFORCE YOUR SKILLS 4.1

Manage Your Customers & Jobs List

In this exercise, you will create, edit, and delete Customers & Jobs List entries for Susie.

Edit a Customer Record

1. Open the Customer Center by choosing **Customers→Customer Center** from the menu bar.

2. **Double-click** Lisa Mills to open it for editing.

3. Change the customer's name to **Lisa Silvers**.
   You will have to change the name in five separate locations. You can use the Copy button to copy the Bill to Address to the Ship to Address field. This customer's name will change in all of the transactions that Lisa was involved in, as well as in all of her future transactions.

4. Click **OK** to accept the change.

Add a New Customer

5. Click the **New Customer & Job** button and choose **New Customer**.

6. Use the following information to set up the new customer, making sure to select the correct tab to enter each piece of information:

Name	Karen Douglas
Address	4673 South Stayton Way, San Marcos, CA 92069
Phone	760-555-8137
Fax	760-555-8237
Type	Catering
Terms	Net 15
Account Number	214

7. Click **OK** to accept the new record.

Delete a Customer Record

8. **Single-click** Andy Freston to select the name.

9. Choose **Edit→Delete Customer:Job** from the menu bar.

10. Click **OK** to confirm the deletion.

11. Close the **Customer Center** window.

Work with Service and Sales Tax Items

In this exercise, you will set up sales tax and service items for Susie.

Turn On Sales Tax Preference and Create a Sales Tax Item

You must first turn on the sales tax preference and set up a sales tax item.

1. Choose **Edit→Preferences** from the menu bar.

2. Display the **Company Preferences** tab of the Sales Tax category.

3. Turn on the **sales tax preference**.

4. Set up a new sales tax item using the following information:

Sales Tax Name	SD County
Description	San Diego County Sales Tax
Tax Rate	8.25%
Tax Agency	San Diego County Treasurer (Quick Add as a vendor)

5. Click **OK** to add the new sales tax item.

6. Choose **SD County** as the most common sales tax item.

7. Click **OK** to close the Preferences window and accept the new preference.

8. Click **OK** in the Updating Sales Tax window; then, click **OK** to acknowledge the closing of all open windows.

Create and Edit Service Items

Remember, you must create items before you can use them on sales forms. It may seem strange, but a restaurant is technically considered a service business! Susie will be adding a catering service to her business, so you will set up the item for her now.

9. Open the Item List by choosing **Lists→Item List**.

10. Click the **Item** menu button and choose **New** from the drop-down menu.

11. Create the following service item:

Item Name	Catering
Description	Off-site Event Catering
Rate	[Leave this blank; you will fill it in for each job]
Account	Catering Sales

12. Click **OK** to accept the new item and close the window.

13. Close the **Item List**.

Enter Sales Transactions

In this exercise, you will create invoices and sales receipts for the Tea Shoppe.

Create an Invoice

You will first enter an invoice for a catering job.

1. Open the Create Invoices window by choosing **Customers→Create Invoices** from the menu bar.

2. Choose **Karen Douglas** as the customer.

3. Set the date to read **6/3/2011**, and then choose to use the **Intuit Service Invoice Template**.

4. Click in the **Item** column of the invoice and choose **Catering** as the item.

5. Tap Tab three times, and then type **$750** in the Rate column.

6. Tap Tab; click **OK** in the Price Level/Billing Rate Level window, if necessary.

7. Select **"We appreciate your prompt payment"** in the Customer Message field.

8. Click **Save & Close** to record the transaction and close the Create Invoices window.

9. Click **No** in the QuickBooks Information window about the Payment Interview, if necessary, choosing to not display the message in the future.

Enter a Sales Receipt

Now you will enter a sales receipt to account for the food and beverage sales.

10. Open the Enter Sales Receipts window by choosing **Customers→Enter Sales Receipts** from the menu bar.

11. Set the date to read **6/4/2011**.

12. Click the **Item** column of the sales receipt and choose **Food** as the item.

13. Enter **$804** as the rate.

14. Click in the **Item** column below the Food entry, and choose **Beverages** as the item.

15. Enter **$1594** as the rate.
    Your sales receipt should match the following figure.

Item	Description	Qty	Rate	Amount	Tax
Food	Weekly Food Sales			804.00	804.00	Non
Beverage	Weekly Beverage Sales			1,594.00	1,594.00	Non

16. Enter the following food and beverage sales for the month of June:
    - 6/11/11: Food **$881**; Beverage: **$1,633**
    - 6/18/11: Food **$871**; Beverage **$1,617**
    - 6/25/11: Food **$865**; Beverage **$1,629**

17. Click **Save & Close** to record the transaction and close the Enter Sales Receipts window.

Receive Payments and Pay Sales Tax

In this exercise, you will receive the payment for the invoice you created earlier and pay all sales tax you have collected.

Receive a Customer's Payment

1. Choose **Customers→Receive Payments** from the menu bar.
2. Choose **Karen Douglas** from the Received From field.
3. Enter **$811.88** for the amount.
4. Set the date to read **6/11/2011**.
5. The payment was written on check number **592**.
6. Click **Save & Close**.

Pay Sales Tax

7. Choose **Vendors→Sales Tax→Pay Sales Tax** from the menu bar.
8. Ensure **Checking** is the account from which the payment will come.
9. Set the **Check Date** and **Show sales tax due** through as **6/30/11**.
10. Choose for the check to be **printed**, and to pay all tax due.
11. Click **OK** to send the liability check to the queue to be printed.

Run Customer-Related and P&L Reports

In this exercise, you will run three reports for Susie: a customer QuickReport, a customer list report, and a profit and loss report.

Create a QuickReport

1. Open the **Customer Center**.
2. **Single-click** Karen Douglas to select it.
3. Click the **QuickReport** link at the far right of the window.
4. Set the date range to **All**.
   You will see a report that shows all of the transactions for Karen Douglas.
5. Choose **Window→Close All** from the menu bar.

Create a List Report and Edit a Customer Record

6. Choose **Reports→Customers & Receivables→Customer Phone List** from the menu bar.

7. Using your QuickZoom pointer, **double-click** Karen Douglas.
   QuickBooks will open an Edit Customer window, from where you can make any changes to the customer's information.

8. Change Karen's phone number to **760-555-8037**; click **OK**.

9. Choose **Window→Close All** from the menu bar.

Create a Profit & Loss Report

10. Choose **Reports→Company & Financial→Profit & Loss Standard**.

11. Type **a** to set the date range to **All**.

12. Close the report, choosing not to memorize it.

13. Choose the appropriate option for your situation:
    - If you are continuing on to the next lesson or the rest of the end-of-lesson exercises, leave QuickBooks open.
    - If you are finished working in QuickBooks for now, choose **File→Exit** from the menu bar.

Apply Your Skills

Before you begin these exercises, restore the Wet Noses Veterinary Clinic Lesson 4 (Portable) file or open the file that you used for the Apply Your Skills exercise in Lesson 3. Name the file [Your Name]'s Wet Noses Vet Clinic. If you need to review how to restore a portable company file, follow steps 1–8 in Develop Your Skills 3.1.1.

APPLY YOUR SKILLS 4.1

Set Up a Customers & Jobs List

In this exercise, you will work on the Customers & Jobs List for Wet Noses. If you wish, you may explore the Add/Edit Multiple List Entries feature and use it to complete this exercise. It will be fully introduced in QuickBooks Pro 2011: Level 2.

1. Open the **Customer Center**.

2. Set up the following customers for Wet Noses Veterinary Clinic:

Name	Edison York	LaShonda Reeves	Ellie Sanders
Address	7931 NE 176th St. Bothell, WA 98011	11908 100th Pl. NE Kirkland, WA 98034	302 Northshore Blvd. Bothell, WA 98011
Phone	425-555-4401	425-555-3953	425-555-7731
Type	From advertisement	Referral	From advertisement
Terms	Due on receipt	Due on receipt	Due on receipt
Account Number	C94	D22	D34
Pet Type & Name (Create as a Job for each customer)	Dog-Hummer	Cat-Squeakers	Dog-Sully

3. Close the **Customer Center**.

Set Up Items

In this exercise, you will set up service and sales tax items.

Prepare to Track Sales Tax

We will assume that a new law went into effect requiring Wet Noses to collect sales tax on inventory and non-inventory items as of June 1, 2011. (This is an assumption for the purpose of learning to use the sales tax feature in QuickBooks and not a true statement in regards to sales tax in the state of Washington. You must find out from your local agency what laws apply to your business in regards to collecting and remitting sales tax). You will help Dr. James to set up to collect sales tax on these types of items. Service items will remain nontaxable.

1. Open the **Preferences** window and set the preference to collect sales tax.

2. Set up a new **sales tax item**, King County Sales Tax for 10%, payable to King County Treasurer, and then set it as the most common sales tax item.

3. Click **OK** to close the Preferences window and accept the new preference.

4. Choose to make all existing customers taxable but not all existing non-inventory and inventory parts.

Set Up Service and Non-Inventory Items

5. Set up the following service items:

Item Name	**Boarding**	**Dental**
Description	**Overnight Boarding**	**Dental Cleaning**
Rate	**35.00**	**45.00**
Account	**Nonmedical Income**	**Fee for Service Income**
Tax Code	**None**	**None**

6. Set up the following non-inventory item:

Item Name	**Treats**
Description	**Treats for patients—by the box**
Rate	**18.43**
Account	**Boarding Food & Supplies**
Tax Code	**Tax**

7. Close the **Item List** window.

Work with Customer Transactions and Pay Sales Tax

In this exercise, you will complete sales transactions and receive payments for Wet Noses' customers. Remember that you will collect sales tax on non-inventory items but not on service items.

Record Sales Transactions

You will start by helping Dr. James to record invoices and cash sales. Enter the sales information and update the Additional Info tab for the job to capture the custom field information for each pet.

1. On 6/1/11, Emily Dallas brought her male black lab, Cowboy, in for an Exam, Vaccine Injection Fee, and Rabies Vaccine. Invoice her for this and enter her pet's information on the Additional Info tab of her customer record. Collect King County Sales Tax for the vaccine.

2. On 6/2/11, Kimberly Wurn brought her female calico cat (the breed is domestic short hair, or DSH), Princess, in for a New Patient Exam, Vaccine Injection Fee, Feline DHC, and FIV/FeLV. She paid cash, so create a sales receipt for her and enter her pet's information on the Additional Info tab of her customer record. Collect King County Sales Tax for vaccine and test.

3. On 6/3/11, Becky Todd brought her black and white male Jack Russell Terrier dog, Jedi, in for an Exam requiring Venipuncture, ACTH Stimulation Test, CBC Chem, and a Kennel fee. Create an invoice for her and enter her pet's information on the Additional Info tab of her customer record. Collect King County Sales Tax for the appropriate part of this transaction.

4. On 6/4/11, Millie Schumann brought her male orange and white domestic short hair kitten, Smelly, in for an Exam and Pre-A Blood Work. She paid cash, so create a sales receipt for her. Collect King County Sales Tax for the appropriate part of this transaction.

Accept Customer Payments

You will now receive the payments for customer invoices that have been recorded.

5. On 6/7/11, you received check #773 for $58.10 from Emily Dallas as payment for invoice #173.

6. On 6/8/11, you received check #2310 for $284.21 from the County Animal Shelter as payment for invoice #163.

Pay Sales Tax

You will now help Sadie to pay the sales tax that she collected.

7. Choose **Vendors→Sales Tax→Pay Sales Tax** from the menu bar.

8. Set the Check Date and Show sales tax due through as **6/30/11**, ensuring that Checking is the payment account.

9. Choose for the check to be printed, and to pay all tax due.

10. Click **OK** to send the liability check to the queue to be printed.

Answer Questions with Reports

In this exercise, you will answer questions for Dr. James by running reports. You may wish to display the Report Center in List View to help you answer the questions. Ask your instructor if you should print the reports or simply display them on the screen.

1. How much did Sadie's company make during the month of May?

2. Are there any unpaid invoices?

3. What transactions has Wet Noses had with each customer?

4. What transactions make up each customer's current balance?

5. What are the prices for each item?
   Hint: One report will show them all.

6. Choose the appropriate option for your situation:
   - If you are continuing on to the next lesson or the Critical Thinking exercises, leave QuickBooks open.
   - If you are finished working in QuickBooks for now, choose **File→Exit** from the menu bar.

Critical Thinking

In the course of working through the following Critical Thinking exercises, you will be utilizing various skills taught in this and previous lesson(s). Take your time and think carefully about the tasks presented to you. Turn back to the lesson content if you need assistance.

4.1 Sort Through the Stack

Before You Begin: Restore the Monkey Business Lesson 4 (Portable) file from your storage location. (Remember that the password is blank for Mary!)

You have been hired by Mary Minard to help her with her organization's books. She is the owner of Monkey Business, a nonprofit organization that provides low-income students with help in preparing for college placement exams and applying for scholarships. You have just sat down at her desk and found a pile of papers. It is your job to sort through the papers and make sense of what you find, entering information into QuickBooks whenever appropriate, and answering any other questions in a word-processing document saved as **Critical Thinking 4-1**.

- Sticky note: We now also receive funding from the Hanson Family Trust. Would we set them up as a customer? The information for the trust is 900 SE Commercial St., Salem, OR 97306; 503.555.9331; contact, Richard Hanson.

- A handwritten note: We will be providing SAT Prep services to private schools and organizations to raise additional funds for the organization. Can we set up a service item directed to 47250•Service to Outside Orgs? (You will need to set this account up as a subaccount for 47200•Program Income.) Set the amount to zero as it will be entered at the time of "sale."

- Note: How would we set up the students who participate in our program? They don't pay us money, so are they customers or is there another list we can include them on? Enter the following students when you find an answer: Leslie Goldsmith, Greg Harrison, Taylor Morrissey, and Sampson Disher.

- Scribbled on a scrap of paper: Provided an SAT Prep seminar on 7/9/2011 at St. Martin's Catholic School, received check #3821 for $1,100. Can we enter this receipt of cash into QuickBooks?

- A letter from the House Foundation: They will be providing a $5,000 grant (not yet received) to the organization to work with students from rural schools in Yamhill County. Set up the new customer, who is located at 552 Sheridan Avenue, Yamhill, OR 97148.

- Handwritten invoice: College 101 workshop to be held at Lakeside Christian School on 7/27/2011 for $985. Due Net 15. (Hint: You will need to set up College 101 as an Item directed to 47250-Service to Outside Orgs.)

- Scribbled note from Mary: Can you produce a report for me that shows all of the donors and customers for Monkey Business?

- A handwritten question: I don't have customers, but I do have donors and grants... How do I set them up if QuickBooks just has customers?

4.2 Tackle the Tasks

Now is your chance to work a little more with Chez Devereaux Salon and Spa and apply the skills that you have learned in this lesson to accomplish additional tasks. Restore the Critical Thinking 4.2 portable company file from your file storage location. Then, enter the following tasks.

Add a Customer	Add the following customer: Blaise Kennedy, 1021 Miller St., Minoqua, WI 54548 • 715-555-8921 • Referral • Due on Receipt • # A350 Birthday 6/14/72 • Anniv. 7/22/99
Create Items	Service item: PEDI • Spa Pedicure • $40 • 48800•Nail Services Income. Service item: MSG • Hour Massage • $85 • 48900•Spa Services Income (you will need to set up a new account). Non-inventory item: Brush • Salon Brush • $3.67 • 67400•Salon Supplies, Linens, Laundry. Non-inventory item: Towels • Dozen Color Safe Towels • $15 • Salon Supplies, Linens, Laundry.
Create Invoices	Blaise Kennedy • 5/23/11 • 2 Pedicures • 2 Massages Jane Oliver • 5/25/11 • Manicure • Pedicure • Haircut
Create Sales Receipts	Leesa James • 5/22/11 • Manicure • Color • Haircut • Check #692 Curtis Balando • 5/24/11 • Massage • Cash
Receive Payments	Receive full payment for invoice #3 from Leesa James, Check #1632, 5/23/11 Receive full payment for invoice #5 from Tami Dart, Check #872, 5/25/11
Generate Reports	Create a report that will show the contact information for all of your customers. Create a report that shows the sales tax due through 5/31/11.
Pay Sales Tax	Pay all sales tax due through 5/31/11.

Banking with QuickBooks

LESSON OBJECTIVES

After studying this lesson, you will be able to:

- Create bank accounts
- Make deposits into bank accounts
- Transfer funds
- Manage credit card transactions
- Reconcile accounts
- Work with banking reports
- Understand online banking with QuickBooks

Any business must be able to work with bank accounts and the funds contained within to be able to operate effectively. If you utilize credit cards for your business, you will need to know how to work with them as well. In this lesson, you will learn all about dealing with bank and credit card accounts in QuickBooks, from creating them to running reports about them. You will also have an opportunity to explore a little about banking online with QuickBooks.

Chez Devereaux Salon and Spa

Lisa has been getting comfortable performing the basic vendor and customer transactions in QuickBooks. One of the individuals who rents space at her salon, Bill, is now going to take over the books because Lisa has gotten quite busy with her customers and marketing her new company. Bill will take over creating bank accounts, tracking banking transactions, dealing with credit card transactions, and reconciling both the bank and credit card accounts.

In addition, Bill is interested in exploring how online banking with QuickBooks works.

Chez Devereaux Salon and Spa
Reconciliation Detail
10000 · Checking, Period Ending 05/31/2011

Type	Date	Num	Name	Clr	Amount	Balance
Beginning Balance						0.00
Cleared Transactions						
Checks and Payments - 16 items						
Check	04/29/2011	1097	Office Superstore	✓	-25.31	-25.31
Check	04/30/2011	1098	Allen Brothers Gro...	✓	-54.89	-80.20
Check	04/30/2011	1100	Cranberry Fields M...	✓	-34.00	-114.20
Check	04/30/2011	1099	Belle Magazine	✓	-24.00	-138.20
Bill Pmt -Check	05/11/2011	3001	Hitchcock Property...	✓	-500.00	-638.20
Bill Pmt -Check	05/11/2011	3002	Brooks Family Insu...	✓	-136.54	-774.74
Check	05/12/2011	3000	Stacey's Beauty S...	✓	-248.57	-1,023.31
Check	05/12/2011	1101	Cost Club	✓	-183.46	-1,206.77
Check	05/17/2011	3003	Allen Brothers Gro...	✓	-36.21	-1,242.98
Bill Pmt -Check	05/18/2011	3007	Office Superstore	✓	-232.16	-1,475.14
Bill Pmt -Check	05/18/2011	3005	Hitchcock Property...	✓	-200.00	-1,675.14
Bill Pmt -Check	05/18/2011	3004	Brooks Family Insu...	✓	-164.78	-1,839.92
Bill Pmt -Check	05/18/2011	3008	Wisconsin Power ...	✓	-134.28	-1,974.20
Bill Pmt -Check	05/18/2011	3006	Midwest Salon Un...	✓	-63.27	-2,037.47
Transfer	05/30/2011			✓	-5,000.00	-7,037.47
Check	05/31/2011			✓	-10.00	-7,047.47
Total Checks and Payments					-7,047.47	-7,047.47
Deposits and Credits - 3 items						
Transfer	04/29/2011			✓	20,432.67	20,432.67
Deposit	05/26/2011			✓	898.20	21,330.87
Deposit	05/28/2011			✓	100.00	21,430.87
Total Deposits and Credits					21,430.87	21,430.87
Total Cleared Transactions					14,383.40	14,383.40
Cleared Balance					14,383.40	14,383.40
Uncleared Transactions						
Checks and Payments - 4 items						
Sales Tax Paym...	05/31/2011		Wisconsin State T...		-54.20	-54.20
Sales Tax Paym...	05/31/2011		Wisconsin State T...		-26.45	-80.65
Sales Tax Paym...	05/31/2011		Oneida County Tre...		-2.66	-83.31
Sales Tax Paym...	05/31/2011		Oneida County Tre...		-2.43	-85.74
Total Checks and Payments					-85.74	-85.74
Total Uncleared Transactions					-85.74	-85.74
Register Balance as of 05/31/2011					14,297.66	14,297.66
Ending Balance					14,297.66	14,297.66

The Reconciliation Detail report displays all of the transactions that have cleared the bank during the statement period and those that are still outstanding, as well as that the balance at the bank and in QuickBooks match.

5.1 Creating Bank Accounts

The accounts you will work with in this lesson are assets (bank accounts) and liabilities (credit cards). There are two types of bank accounts you will deal with: Checking and Savings. Petty cash accounts will be covered in *QuickBooks Pro 2011: Level 2*.

Accessing Banking Activities in QuickBooks

The banking area on the Home page displays task icons for many of the activities you will perform in this lesson. The rest of the activities can be accessed via the menu bar.

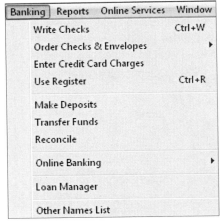

Notice that you can begin the reconciliation process by either clicking the task icon in the Banking area of the Home page or by choosing an option from the menu bar. However, to transfer funds and perform online banking activities, you must use the menu bar.

The Chart of Accounts

Remember from Lesson 2, Creating a Company that the Chart of Accounts is composed of all of the asset, liability, equity, income, and expense accounts your company utilizes. In that lesson, you learned how to create new accounts, edit existing accounts, and delete unused accounts. QuickBooks responds differently when you double-click items in the Chart of Accounts, depending on the type of account, as explained in the following table.

When you double-click this type of account...	QuickBooks responds by...
Any balance sheet account (asset, liability, or equity)	Opening an account register for that account (Exception: The Retained Earnings account, which is a specially created account without a register; you will get a QuickReport when you double-click this account)
Any income or expense account	Creating an account QuickReport

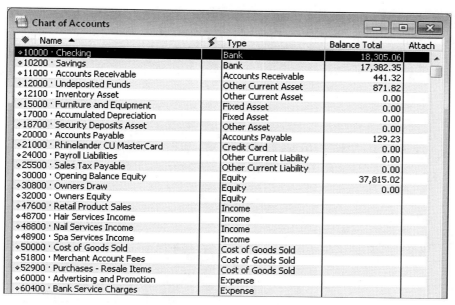

The Chart of Accounts window displays all accounts for a company. Notice that QuickBooks displays a balance for all balance sheet accounts (assets, liabilities, and equity), but not for income, cost of goods sold, and expense accounts. The accounts are listed alphabetically *by type* (unless you have manually rearranged them). The highlighted account (in this case, Checking) is the selected account. It will be affected if you issue a command using the menu buttons at the bottom of the window.

Creating and Editing Accounts

You have already learned the basics regarding creating and editing accounts in the Chart of Accounts. In this lesson, you will look specifically at the basic accounts used in banking: Bank and Credit Card. Remember that you will use the same editing techniques used in a word-processing program to edit account information.

This link, when clicked, launches a Help window to assist you in choosing the correct type of account to create.

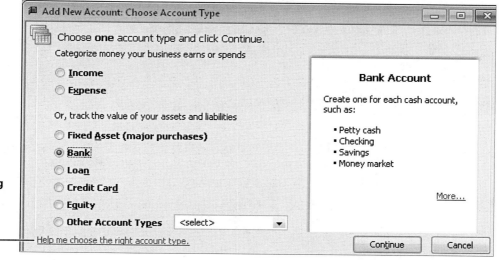

The Add New Account window will help to ensure that you choose the correct type of account when creating a new one. Notice how, when an account type is selected on the left, you see a description of how it is used on the right to assist you in choosing the correct type.

Working with an Account Register

Each balance sheet account (except for Retained Earnings) has its own register, which is a record of all transactions pertaining to the account. A QuickBooks register looks like the check register you may already keep for your personal checking account. The running balance automatically recalculates as you record each new transaction.

When you double-click within a transaction in a register, QuickBooks takes you to the source of the transaction (similar to the QuickZoom feature). For instance, if you double-click the check transaction for Chaparral Office Supply in the following illustration, QuickBooks opens the Write Checks window with all information for the transaction displayed.

Date	Number	Payee		Payment	✓	Deposit	Balance
	Type	Account	Memo				
05/18/2011	3006	Midwest Salon Unlimited		63.27			18,761.64
	BILLPMT	20000 · Accounts I PR203X					
05/18/2011	3007	Office Superstore		232.16			18,529.48
	BILLPMT	20000 · Accounts I 37661P2					
05/18/2011	3008	Wisconsin Power and Gas		134.28			18,395.20
	BILLPMT	20000 · Accounts I Q3029NM5					
05/31/2011	To Print	Oneida County Treasurer		2.96			18,392.24
	TAXPMT	25500 · Sales Tax					

Notice that each transaction in the register includes two lines. The header at the top consists of two lines and describes what is found in each field.

QUICK REFERENCE	WORKING WITH BANKING ACCOUNTS
Task	**Procedure**
Open an account register	■ Open the Chart of Accounts. ■ Double-click the balance sheet account for the register you wish to view.

DEVELOP YOUR SKILLS 5.1.1
Work with Banking Accounts

In this exercise, you will help Bill work with banking accounts and view a register.

Open a Portable Company File
You will start by opening a portable company file.

1. Launch **QuickBooks**.

   You may also continue to use the company file that you worked with in the Critical Thinking 4.2 section of Lesson 4 (make sure you use only the file from Critical Thinking 4.2, not Develop Your Skills). If you choose this option, open the company file in QuickBooks, and then skip to step 5.

2. Choose **File→Open or Restore Company** from the menu bar.

3. Open the Chez Devereaux Salon and Spa Lesson 5 (Portable) file in your default storage location, placing your name as the first word in the filename (e.g., Lisa's Chez Devereaux Salon and Spa).

4. Click **OK** to close the QuickBooks Information window; click **No** in the Set Up External Accountant User window, if necessary.

Edit an Existing Account

5. Click the **Chart of Accounts** task icon in the Company area of the Home page.

6. Follow these steps to edit the account:

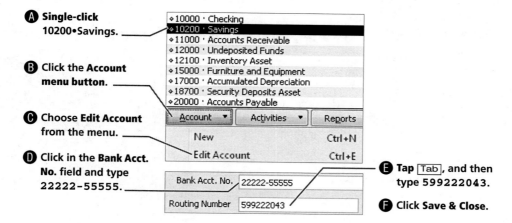

Ⓐ **Single-click 10200•Savings.**

Ⓑ **Click the Account menu button.**

Ⓒ **Choose Edit Account from the menu.**

Ⓓ **Click in the Bank Acct. No. field and type 22222–55555.**

Ⓔ **Tap** `Tab`**, and then type 599222043.**

Ⓕ **Click Save & Close.**

Create a New Account

You will now create a new credit card account that will be used later in this lesson. The Chart of Accounts window should still be open. If it isn't, choose Lists→Chart of Accounts from the menu bar.

7. Click the **Account** menu button, and then choose **New**.

8. Follow these steps to create the new credit card account:

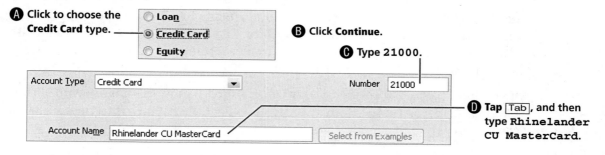

Ⓐ **Click to choose the Credit Card type.**

Ⓑ **Click Continue.**

Ⓒ **Type 21000.**

Ⓓ **Tap** `Tab`**, and then type Rhinelander CU MasterCard.**

9. Click **Save & Close**; click **No** in the Set Up Online Services window.

Open and View a Register

10. **Double-click** Checking in the Chart of Accounts window.

11. Follow these steps to view the original form on which a transaction was entered:

Ⓐ Scroll up until check number **3008** is visible.

Ⓑ Double-click anywhere within the two lines of the transaction.

Date	Number	Payee		Payment	✓	Deposit	Balance
	Type	Account	Memo				
05/18/2011	3006	Midwest Salon Unlimited		63.27			18,761.64
	BILLPMT	20000 · Accounts I PR203X					
05/18/2011	3007	Office Superstore		232.16			18,529.48
	BILLPMT	20000 · Accounts I 37661P2					
05/18/2011	3008	Wisconsin Power and Gas		134.28			18,395.20
	BILLPMT	20000 · Accounts I Q3029NM5					
05/31/2011	To Print	Oneida County Treasurer		2.96			18,392.24
	TAXPMT	25500 · Sales Tax					

QuickBooks will take you to the Bill Payments (Check) – Checking window.

12. Choose **Window→Close All** from the menu bar.

5.2 Making Deposits

If you have utilized the Undeposited Funds account (as you did in the last lesson), you will need to take one more step to move your payments to your bank account. This step is accomplished through the Make Deposits window. The Make Deposits window can also be used when you make a sale and do not need a sales receipt, or when you want to deposit a lump sum that will credit an income account and debit your bank account.

If you have payments sitting in your Undeposited Funds account and you click the Record Deposits task icon on the Home page, you will get the Payments to Deposit window. Here you can choose which payments you wish to deposit.

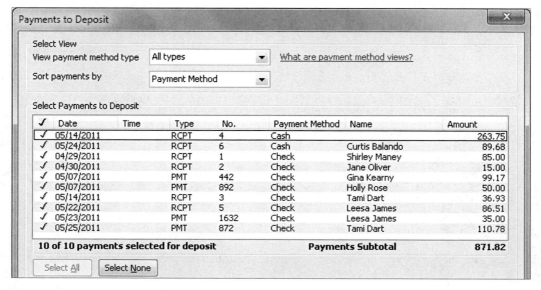

The Payments to Deposit window

You can always click OK if you are not ready to deposit the payments shown in the Payments to Deposit window yet still need to work with the Make Deposits window.

By clicking this drop-down arrow, you can select any bank account that you have set up in QuickBooks.

If you wish to keep cash back from the deposit, you can indicate that in this portion of the window. You will learn more about working with petty cash in Lesson 4, Working with Balance Sheet Accounts and Budgets.

The Memo fields are optional, but keep in mind that you can display your memos on reports.

Make Deposits

Previous | Next | Save | Print | Payments | History | Journal | Attach

Deposit To 10000 · Ch...   Date 05/26/2011   Memo Deposit

Click Payments to select customer payments that you have received. List any other amounts to deposit below.

Received From	From Account	Memo	Chk No.	Pmt Meth.	Amount
	12000 · Undeposited Funds			Cash	263.75
Curtis Balando	12000 · Undeposited Funds			Cash	89.68
Shirley Maney	12000 · Undeposited Funds		2639	Check	85.00
Jane Oliver	12000 · Undeposited Funds		325	Check	15.00
Gina Kearny	12000 · Undeposited Funds		442	Check	99.17
Holly Rose	12000 · Undeposited Funds		892	Check	50.00
Tami Dart	12000 · Undeposited Funds		1539	Check	36.93
Leesa James	12000 · Undeposited Funds		692	Check	86.51
Leesa James	12000 · Undeposited Funds		1632	Check	35.00

Deposit Subtotal 871.82

To get cash back from this deposit, enter the amount below. Indicate the account where you want this money to go, such as your Petty Cash account.

Cash back goes to	Cash back memo	Cash back amount

Deposit Total 871.82

The Make Deposits window. You can click the Print button to print a detailed report of your deposits, including deposit slips if you choose to purchase and use them.

BEHIND THE SCENES

If you make deposits from your Undeposited Funds account, the following accounting will occur behind the scenes.

12000-Undeposited Funds		10000-Checking	
Bal. 871.82		871.82	
	871.82		
0.00			

If you use the Make Deposits window to record sales, the accounting involved is as follows.

48800-Nail Services Income		10000-Checking	
	100	100	

Task	Procedure
Make a deposit from the Undeposited Funds account	■ Choose Banking→Make Deposits from the menu bar. ■ Choose the payment(s) you wish to deposit, and then click OK. ■ Choose the correct bank account and date for the deposit. ■ Click Save & Close or Save & New.
Make a deposit directly to a bank account	■ Choose Banking→Make Deposits from the menu bar; click OK if the Payments to Deposit window appears. ■ Choose the correct bank account and date for the deposit. ■ Enter all of the deposit information including the customer (if desired), account, payment method, and amount. ■ Click Save & Close or Save & New.

Use the Make Deposits Window

In this exercise, you will work with the Make Deposits window to deposit funds from the Undeposited Funds account and to make a deposit without a sales form.

Deposit Funds from the Undeposited Funds Account

1. Click the **Home** button on the icon bar.

2. Click the **Record Deposits** task icon in the Banking area of the Home page.

3. Click the **Select All** button; QuickBooks will place a checkmark to the left of all ten payments waiting to be deposited.

Notice that after you click the Select All button, it is grayed out. It is no longer a valid selection since all payments are already selected.

4. Click **OK** to accept the payments for deposit and move on to the Make Deposits window.

5. Click the drop-down arrow for the **Deposit To** field, and then choose **10000•Checking**; click **OK** in the Setting Default Accounts window, if necessary.

6. Tap Tab, and then type **052611** as the date.

7. Click the **Save & New** button to make the deposit to your Checking account. Leave the Make Deposits window open for the next step.
   Your insertion point should be in the Deposit To field of a clear Make Deposits window. If this is not the case, choose Banking→Make Deposits from the menu bar.

Make a Deposit Without Specifying a Customer

Lisa worked at a church fundraiser and provided $20 manicures, for which she received $10 for each one and donated the remaining $10. Since there were multiple customers whom she does not want to track individually, she will make a deposit to Checking, directly crediting Nail Services Income.

8. Tap [Tab] to move to the Date field.

9. Follow these steps to complete the deposit:

Ⓐ **Tap ⊞ until the date reads 5/28/11.**   Ⓑ **Tap [Tab], and then type Church Fundraiser.**

Deposit To	10000 · Ch... ▼	Date	05/28/2011 📅	Memo	Church Fundraiser

Click Payments to select customer payments that you have received. List any other amounts to deposit below.

Received From	From Account	Memo	Chk No.	Pmt Meth.	Amount
	48800 · Nail Services Income			Cash	100.00

Ⓒ **Tap [Tab] twice, and then type n to choose Nail Services Income as the account.**   Ⓓ **Tap [Tab] three times, and then type c to choose Cash.**   Ⓔ **Tap [Tab], and then type 100 as the amount.**

Note that you don't fill in an item in this form, but you do fill in the account. Remember that an item is used to direct funds to the underlying account. You cannot leave the From Account field blank because you must specify the account that will be credited since you will be debiting a bank account with the deposit.

10. Click **Save & Close**; your deposit will be recorded, and the window will close.

5.3 Transferring Funds

Most people have transferred money between their bank accounts. QuickBooks has a feature that allows you to record this transfer. If you use online banking, you can even set QuickBooks to perform the transfer for you when you go online.

Since you are transferring funds between two asset accounts, you want to debit the account that is increasing and credit the account that is decreasing. Look at the following T-accounts to visualize this transaction.

FLASHBACK TO GAAP: MONETARY UNIT

Remember that it is assumed a stable currency is going to be the unit of record.

BEHIND THE SCENES

In this illustration, you are transferring funds from the Checking account to the Savings account.

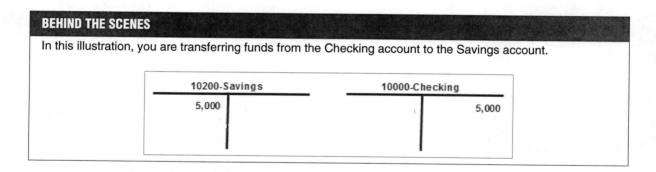

QUICK REFERENCE	TRANSFERRING FUNDS BETWEEN ACCOUNTS
Task	**Procedure**
Transfer funds	■ Choose Banking→Transfer Funds from the menu bar.
	■ Choose the account from which you wish to draw the funds.
	■ Choose the account to which you wish to send the funds.
	■ Type the amount to be transferred and, if you wish, a memo.
	■ Click Save & Close or Save & New to record the transfer.

DEVELOP YOUR SKILLS 5.3.1
Transfer Funds Between Accounts

In this exercise, Bill will transfer funds between the Checking and Savings accounts.

1. Choose **Banking→Transfer Funds** from the menu bar.

2. Follow these steps to complete the funds transfer:

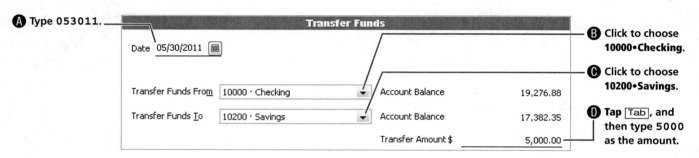

A Type 053011.

B Click to choose **10000•Checking.**

C Click to choose **10200•Savings.**

D Tap Tab, and then type **5000** as the amount.

Notice that QuickBooks displays the account balances of the accounts involved in the transfer so you can verify sufficient funds are available.

3. Click **Save & Close** to record the transaction.

5.4 Managing Credit and Debit Card Transactions

Credit cards give business owners an easy way to track their expenses. QuickBooks allows you to track credit card transactions just as you track checking and savings account transactions. You can set up as many credit card accounts as you need; then, simply choose the account you want to work with in the Enter Credit Card Charges window.

If you use your personal credit cards occasionally for business purposes, you should not enter them in QuickBooks as business credit cards. Only create accounts for business credit cards.

Credit card transactions are classified as either a charge (when you make a purchase) or a credit (when you make a return). As you will use the same form for both types, you need to choose the correct type when entering transactions.

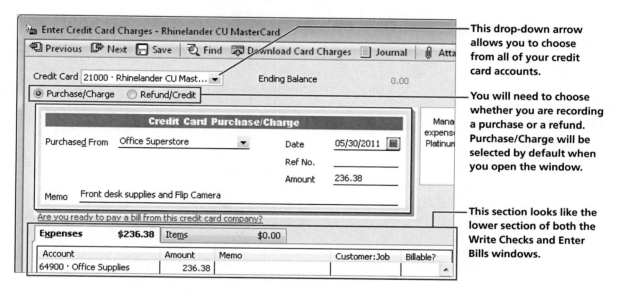

This drop-down arrow allows you to choose from all of your credit card accounts.

You will need to choose whether you are recording a purchase or a refund. Purchase/Charge will be selected by default when you open the window.

This section looks like the lower section of both the Write Checks and Enter Bills windows.

Type of Account and Normal Balance

A credit card is a liability, so its normal balance is a credit. This means you credit the account when you make a purchase (a "charge") and debit the account when you make a payment (a "credit").

The term credit is a bit confusing at this point, as you will debit your credit card account if you enter a "credit" transaction. However, if you think of it from the perspective of the merchant, it makes perfect sense!

Pay a Bill with a Credit Card

If you have entered a bill into QuickBooks, you do have the option to pay it with a credit card. Make sure that you use the Pay Bills window to accomplish the task, though, as you must remove the amount from Accounts Payable!

If you use the Enter Credit Card charges window to pay a bill that you entered through the QuickBooks Enter Bills window, you must use the Pay Bills window when you pay it!

Dealing with Debit Card Transactions

When you make a purchase or pay a bill with a debit card, funds are taken directly from your checking account, which is different than what occurs for credit card purchases. Use the Write Checks window to handle debit card transactions. If you use the Enter/Pay Bills windows in QuickBooks, you can continue to use them when working with debit card purchases. This means that if you have entered a bill in QuickBooks and then choose to use a debit card to pay it, you must enter that payment through the Pay Bills window. Otherwise, the expenses will be overstated and you will leave the bill hanging out in Accounts Payable.

When you enter a debit card transaction in the Write Checks window, indicate it by entering a code such as "DB" in the No. field.

Other Types of Transactions Affecting the Checking Account

In addition to debit card transactions, you may have other ones that draw funds from the checking account as well. For instance, ATM cards and a service such as PayPal can directly withdraw funds from your bank account. All of these transactions will be entered using the Write Checks window; you just need to create common codes that will be used in the No. field to record each type of transaction. Common codes include DB for debit card, ATM for an ATM card transaction, and PP for a PayPal payment. You do not have to use the codes suggested here; however, you should choose one code for each type of transaction and stick with it!

A purchase credits the credit card account, as shown here.

21000-Rhinelander CU MasterCard		64900-Office Supplies	
	236.38	236.38	

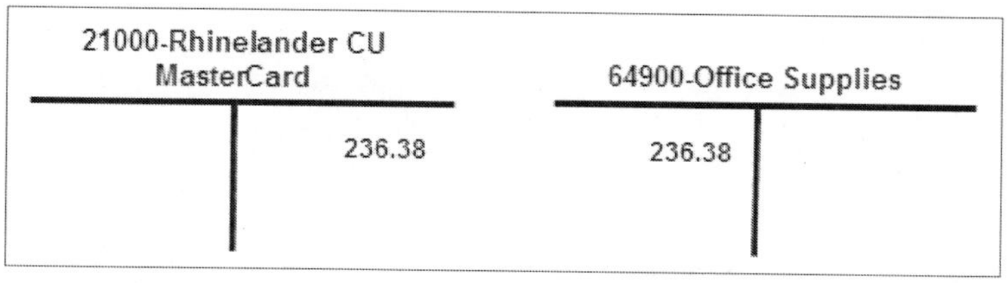

A payment debits the credit card account, as shown here.

21000-Rhinelander CU MasterCard		10000-Checking	
195.35			195.35

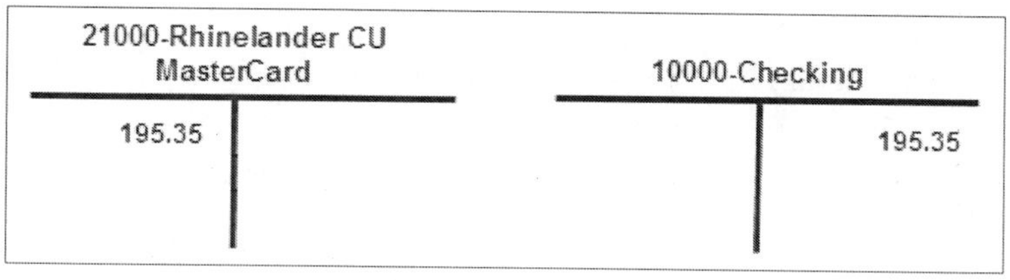

When you use a credit card to pay a bill, the following occurs behind the scenes for you.

21000-Rhinelander CU MasterCard		20000-Accounts Payable	
	129.23	129.23	

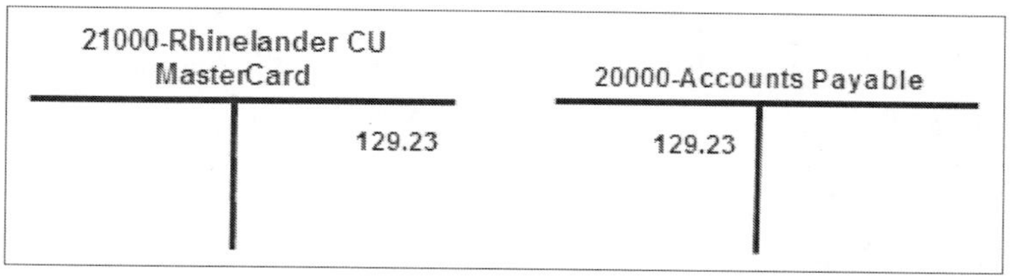

When you use a debit card to purchase office supplies, the following occurs behind the scenes for you.

64900-Office Supplies		10000-Checking	
100.00			100.00

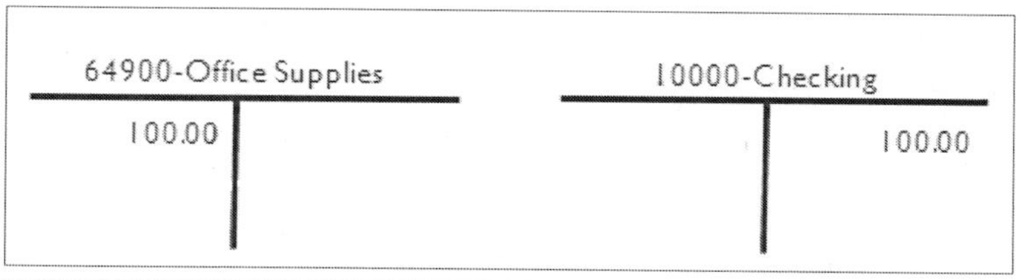

Task	Procedure
Record a credit card transaction	■ Choose Banking→Enter Credit Card Charges from the menu bar. ■ Choose the account to record a purchase or refund to. ■ Enter the transaction information. ■ Click Save & Close or Save & New.
Record a debit card transaction	■ Choose Banking→Write Checks from the menu bar. ■ Select the bank account to which the debit card is linked. ■ Enter "DB" or the code you have chosen in the No. field. ■ Enter information into the payee, amount, and memo fields. ■ Ensure the proper expense or asset accounts are indicated on the Expense and/or Item tab at the bottom of the window. ■ Click Save & Close or Save & New.
Record a debit card transaction for a bill entered already entered into Accounts Payable	■ Choose Vendors→Pay Bills from the menu bar. ■ Select the bill you wish to pay by debit card. ■ Set the date and account to which the debit card is linked. ■ Choose to Assign check number in the Payment Method portion of the window, and then click Pay Selected Bills. ■ Type in the code you have chosen to use for debit card purchases (such as "DB") in the Assign Check Numbers window, and then click OK. ■ Click Done in the Payment Summary window.

Manage Credit Card Transactions

In this exercise, you will help Bill enter a credit card purchase and a return, as well as pay a bill with a credit card.

Record a Credit Card Purchase

Lisa needs to purchase some supplies for the front desk. She has also decided to purchase a flip camera so she can start a portfolio of her special event work.

1. Click the **Enter Credit Card Charges** in the Banking area of the Home page.
   Since you only have one credit card set up at this time, the information will fill in to the Credit Card field. If you had multiple cards, you would need to choose the appropriate one before entering other information.

2. Follow these steps to record the credit card charge:

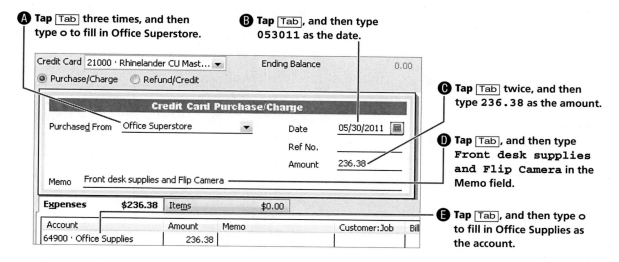

Ⓐ Tap `Tab` **three times, and then type o to fill in Office Superstore.**

Ⓑ Tap `Tab`**, and then type 053011 as the date.**

Ⓒ Tap `Tab` **twice, and then type 236.38 as the amount.**

Ⓓ Tap `Tab`**, and then type Front desk supplies and Flip Camera in the Memo field.**

Ⓔ Tap `Tab`**, and then type o to fill in Office Supplies as the account.**

3. Click the **Save & New** button.

Record a Credit Card Return

In the next transaction, Lisa returns a calculator she purchased at Office Superstore, as she realized she didn't need it once she got back to the salon.

4. Follow these steps to record the credit card refund:

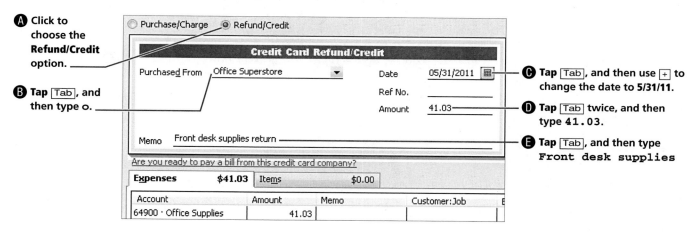

Ⓐ Click to choose the Refund/Credit option.

Ⓑ Tap `Tab`**, and then type o.**

Ⓒ Tap `Tab`**, and then use** `+` **to change the date to 5/31/11.**

Ⓓ Tap `Tab` **twice, and then type 41.03.**

Ⓔ Tap `Tab`**, and then type Front desk supplies**

Notice that the account 64900•Office Supplies fills in for you since that is the account you used last time for this vendor. You can either leave it as is when this occurs or change it to a different account if that is appropriate.

5. Click the **Save & Close** button.
QuickBooks records the transaction and closes the Enter Credit Card Charges window.

Pay a Bill with a Credit Card

You can record a bill paid by credit card in QuickBooks, although you must use the Pay Bills window in order to properly affect Accounts Payable.

6. Click the **Pay Bills** task icon in the Vendors area of the Home page.

7. Follow these steps to pay a bill with a credit card:

Ⓐ Click to place a checkmark in this box.

Ⓑ Set the date to 5/31/11, if necessary.

Ⓒ Choose **Credit Card** as the Method.   Ⓓ Click **Pay Selected Bills.**

Notice that when you choose Credit Card as the method of payment, Rhinelander CU MasterCard automatically fills in as the payment account. If you have multiple credit card accounts, make sure that the correct account is displayed.

8. Click **Done** in the Payment Summary window.

QuickBooks records the bill payment, debiting Accounts Payable and crediting Rhinelander CU MasterCard for you.

It is important to make sure that your account records in QuickBooks match those of the bank. The process of matching your accounts to the bank statements you receive is called *reconciliation*.

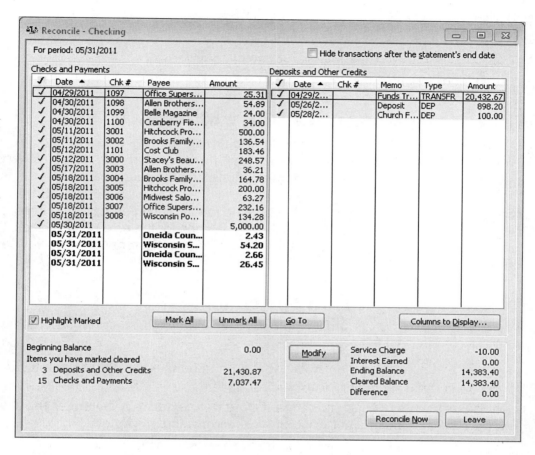

QuickBooks bank account reconciliation window

QuickBooks' Reconciliation Features

You should be aware of some important reconciliation features in QuickBooks. You can save your reconciliation reports in PDF (Portable Document Format) so they are ready to send via email and are viewable with the free Adobe Reader program (also known as Acrobat Reader). In QuickBooks Pro, when you reconcile a new statement, the reconciliation report replaces the prior report with the new month's information. You should save each report as a PDF file to a storage location such as your hard drive or a network drive if you are using the Pro edition. In QuickBooks Premier and Enterprise editions, QuickBooks stores all reconciliation reports as PDF files for you, and you can access them through QuickBooks at any time.

Locating Discrepancies

QuickBooks also provides a feature that helps you locate discrepancies if there is a difference in balances during the reconciliation process. You can run a Reconciliation Discrepancy Report that lists transactions affecting the reconciliation balance. The types of transactions that can affect the balance are:

- Deleted transactions
- A change to a previously cleared amount
- Transactions that were manually un-cleared in the register
- Transactions in which the date was changed to a different statement period

When Your Accounts Don't Match

It is important to take the time when performing reconciliations to ensure there are no errors. As you clear each transaction, make sure the amounts are exactly the same. It is very frustrating when you get to the end of the transactions, and they don't balance.

Once you have cleared transactions through the reconciliation process, it is important to *not* change them. Changes may alter your starting balance for the next reconciliation. If you find yourself in such a situation, you can run a Reconciliation Discrepancy report to find the problem(s).

Problem Resolution Process

If you do find yourself in the unfavorable situation of finishing your reconciliation without balancing, consider the following suggestions:

- Look for a transaction that is exactly the same amount as the difference and ensure whether or not it should be cleared.
- Determine whether you are missing a deposit or a payment by looking at the totals of each on the bank statement and the QuickBooks reconciliation window.
- Compare the number of transactions on the bank statement to the number of cleared transactions in QuickBooks.
- Verify the individual amount of each transaction on the bank statement and compare it to the amounts you have in QuickBooks.
- Determine whether it is a bank error (the bank may have recorded a transaction for the wrong amount). If it is a bank error, you can create an adjustment transaction in Quick-Books, notify the bank, and then reverse the adjustment transaction after the bank corrects the error.
- Run a Reconciliation Discrepancy report to see if any changes were made to previously cleared transactions. If changes were made to previously cleared transactions, undo the last reconciliation and redo it.

Reconciling Credit Cards

You can reconcile your credit cards the same way as you reconcile your bank account, although you access the command through the Chart of Accounts.

Once you have reconciled the credit card, you have the option to pay any amount due. You can choose to either write a check or enter a bill for the payment. QuickBooks takes the balance due on the credit card and fills it in to either the Enter Bills or the Write Checks window. If you don't plan to pay the entire amount owed, you can change the amount manually.

FLASHBACK TO GAAP: ASSUMPTION OF A GOING CONCERN

Remember that it is assumed that the business will be in operation indefinitely.

QUICK REFERENCE	RECONCILING BANK AND CREDIT CARD ACCOUNTS
Task	**Procedure**
Reconcile a bank account	■ Choose Banking→Reconcile from the menu bar.
	■ Choose the account you wish to reconcile; enter the date of the bank statement and the ending balance.
	■ Enter any service or finance charges, and then click Continue.
	■ Compare the QuickBooks transactions to the bank statement; mark off all those that have cleared.
	■ Once the difference between QuickBooks and the bank statement is zero, click Reconcile Now.
Reconcile a credit card	■ Choose Lists→Chart of Accounts from the menu bar; single-click on the credit card account you wish to reconcile.
	■ Click the Activities button at the bottom of the window, and then choose Reconcile Credit Card.
	■ Choose the account; enter the date of the credit card statement and the ending balance.
	■ Enter any service or finance charges, and then click Continue.
	■ Compare the QuickBooks transactions to the bank statement; mark off all those that have cleared.
	■ Once the difference between QuickBooks and the bank statement is zero, click Reconcile Now.

DEVELOP YOUR SKILLS 5.5.1
Reconcile Accounts

In this exercise, you will use the QuickBooks reconciliation tool for both a bank account and a credit card account.

Before You Begin: *You will be working with a bank statement and a credit card statement in this exercise. You can use the illustrations of the statements provided in the book, or you can print them from your file storage location. The files are labeled Develop Your Skills 5.5 Checking Statement and Develop Your Skills 5.5 Credit Card Statement.*

Prepare to Reconcile a Checking Account

First, you will prepare to help Bill reconcile the checking account for Chez Devereaux Salon and Spa. The bank statement for this account that you will use to complete the reconciliation is displayed here.

Silver Falls Credit Union
487 Merrifield Avenue
Rhinelander, WI 54501

Statement of Account Prepared For:
Chez Devereaux Salon and Spa
444 North Pelham St.
Rhinelander, WI 54501

Checking Account Number: 11111-44444

Statement Period: May 1 - May 31, 2011

Total Deposits:	$998.20	Total Payments:	$7,047.47
Beginning Balance:	$20,432.67	Ending Balance:	$14,385.15

Transactions:

Date	Transaction type	Payment	Deposit	Balance
5/1/2011	Beginning Balance			$20,432.67
5/2/2011	Check #1097	25.31		$20,407.36
5/3/2011	Check #1098	54.89		$20,352.47
5/6/2011	Check #1099	24.00		$20,328.47
5/7/2011	Check #1100	34.00		$20,294.47
5/13/2011	Check #3001	500.00		$19,794.47
5/16/2011	Check #3002	136.54		$19,657.93
5/17/2011	Check #1101	183.46		$19,474.47
5/17/2001	Check #3000	248.57		$19,225.90
5/19/2011	Check #3003	36.21		$19,189.69
5/20/2011	Check #3004	164.78		$19,024.91
5/23/2011	Check #3005	200.00		$18,824.91
5/23/2011	Check #3008	134.28		$18,690.63
5/24/2011	Check #3007	232.16		$18,458.47
5/25/2011	Check #3006	63.27		$18,395.20
5/26/2011	Deposit		899.95	$19,295.15
5/30/2011	Deposit		100.00	$19,395.15
5/30/2011	Transfer to Savings	5,000.00		$14,395.15
5/31/2011	Service Charge	10.00		$14,385.15
	Ending Balance			$14,385.15

1. Click the **Reconcile** task icon in the Banking area of the Home page.
   QuickBooks displays the Begin Reconciliation window.

Reconcile

2. Using the illustration of the bank statement provided or the one you printed, follow these steps to prepare for reconciliation:

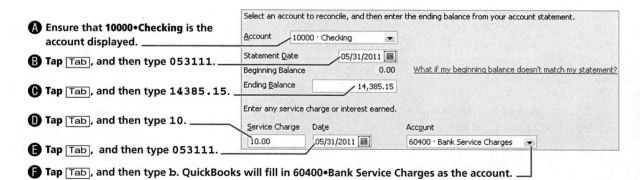

A Ensure that **10000•Checking** is the account displayed.

B Tap Tab, and then type **053111.**

C Tap Tab, and then type **14385.15.**

D Tap Tab, and then type **10.**

E Tap Tab, and then type **053111.**

F Tap Tab, and then type **b**. QuickBooks will fill in 60400•Bank Service Charges as the account.

3. Click **Continue** to move to the Reconciliation-Checking window.
   The Reconciliation-Checking window shows all transactions waiting to be cleared.

Reconcile a Checking Account

Now that you have finished the prep work, it is time to begin the actual reconciliation.

4. Click in the √ (checkmark) column to the left of each transaction in QuickBooks that is also on the bank checking statement displayed above step 1.
   When you are finished, your Reconciliation-Checking window should match the following illustration.

√	Checks and Payments Date ▲	Chk #	Payee	Amount		√	Deposits and Other Credits Date ▲	Chk #	Memo	Type	Amount
√	04/29/2011	1097	Office Supe...	25.31		√	04/29/2...		Funds Tr...	TRANSFR	20,432.67
√	04/30/2011	1098	Allen Broth...	54.89		√	05/26/2...		Deposit	DEP	899.95
√	04/30/2011	1099	Belle Magaz...	24.00		√	05/28/2...		Church F...	DEP	100.00
√	04/30/2011	1100	Cranberry ...	34.00							
√	05/11/2011	3001	Hitchcock P...	500.00							
√	05/11/2011	3002	Brooks Fami...	136.54							
√	05/12/2011	1101	Cost Club	183.46							
√	05/12/2011	3000	Stacey's Be...	248.57							
√	05/17/2011	3003	Allen Broth...	36.21							
√	05/18/2011	3004	Brooks Fami...	164.78							
√	05/18/2011	3005	Hitchcock P...	200.00							
√	05/18/2011	3006	Midwest Sal...	63.27							
√	05/18/2011	3007	Office Supe...	232.16							
√	05/18/2011	3008	Wisconsin P...	134.28							
√	05/30/2011			5,000.00							
	05/31/2011		Oneida Co...	2.43							
	05/31/2011		Wisconsin ...	62.48							
	05/31/2011		Oneida Co...	2.66							
	05/31/2011		Wisconsin ...	26.45							

5. Look at the "Difference" at the bottom right of the window to see if you have successfully reconciled your account.
   The goal when you perform a reconciliation is for the Difference to be 0.00. The Difference is calculated by determining the difference between the transactions on the bank statement and those that you have marked cleared in QuickBooks.

Beginning Balance	0.00		Modify	Service Charge	-10.00
Items you have marked cleared				Interest Earned	0.00
3 Deposits and Other Credits	21,432.62			Ending Balance	14,385.15
15 Checks and Payments	7,037.47			Cleared Balance	14,385.15
				Difference	0.00

6. Click the **Reconcile Now** button; then, click **OK** in the Information window.
   There is a pause as QuickBooks records the marked transactions as cleared.

7. Click **Close** to choose to not produce a report at this time.
   You will learn about reconciliation reports in the next section.

Prepare to Reconcile a Credit Card Account

The process of reconciling a credit card account is quite similar to the process you just used to reconcile a bank statement. You can either use the illustration provided below or the one you may have printed before starting this exercise.

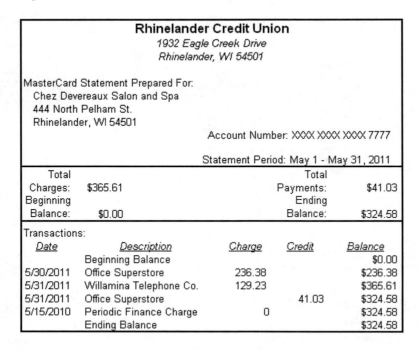

Rhinelander Credit Union
1932 Eagle Creek Drive
Rhinelander, WI 54501

MasterCard Statement Prepared For:
Chez Devereaux Salon and Spa
444 North Pelham St.
Rhinelander, WI 54501

Account Number: XXXX XXXX XXXX 7777

Statement Period: May 1 - May 31, 2011

Total Charges:	$365.61	Total Payments:	$41.03
Beginning Balance:	$0.00	Ending Balance:	$324.58

Transactions:

Date	Description	Charge	Credit	Balance
	Beginning Balance			$0.00
5/30/2011	Office Superstore	236.38		$236.38
5/31/2011	Willamina Telephone Co.	129.23		$365.61
5/31/2011	Office Superstore		41.03	$324.58
5/15/2010	Periodic Finance Charge	0		$324.58
	Ending Balance			$324.58

8. Choose **Lists→Chart of Accounts** from the menu bar.

9. **Single-click** 21000•Rhinelander CU MasterCard to select it.

10. Click the **Activities** button at the bottom of the Chart of Accounts window, and then choose **Reconcile Credit Card** from the menu.

11. Using the credit card you just printed or the illustration provided, follow these steps to prepare for reconciliation:

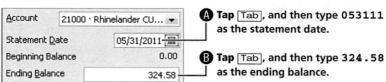

Ⓐ Tap Tab, and then type **053111** as the statement date.

Ⓑ Tap Tab, and then type **324.58** as the ending balance.

12. Click **Continue** to begin reconciling.

Reconcile the Credit Card Account

13. Click in the √ (checkmark) column to the left of each transaction in QuickBooks that is also on the credit card statement displayed above step 8.
When you are finished, your Reconcile Credit Card – Rhinelander CU MasterCard window should match the following illustration.

Charges and Cash Advances					Payments and Credits				
√	Date ▲	R...	Payee	Amount	√	Date ▲	Re...	Memo	Type	Amount
√	05/30/2011		Office Superstore	236.38	√	05/31/2011		Front desk sup...	CC CRED	41.03
√	05/31/2011		Willamina Telephone Comp...	129.23						

14. Look at the "Difference" to see if it is zero.
If you do not have a difference of zero, look back at the Problem Resolution Process section on page 172 for troubleshooting ideas as to how to resolve the difference.

15. Once the Difference is displayed as 0.00, click the **Reconcile Now** button.
QuickBooks will clear all of the marked transactions, and since you have a balance due on the credit card, a Make Payment window will be displayed.

Write a Check to Make a Payment on the Credit Card Account

You can either enter a bill for the payment amount or write a check. You will help Bill to write a check in this exercise.

16. Choose the **Write a check for payment now** option.

17. Click **OK** to continue.
There is a pause as QuickBooks records the cleared transactions. A congratulatory message will appear.

18. Click the **Close** button in the Select Reconciliation Report window to bypass creating a report.
QuickBooks displays the Write Checks – Checking window with much of the information already filled in for you.

> **Make Payment**
>
> The outstanding balance on this account is $324.58. To pay all or a portion of this amount, select the payment type and click OK. To leave the balance in the reconciled account, click Cancel.
>
> Payment
> ⦿ Write a check for payment now
> ○ Enter a bill for payment later

19. Follow these steps to complete the check:

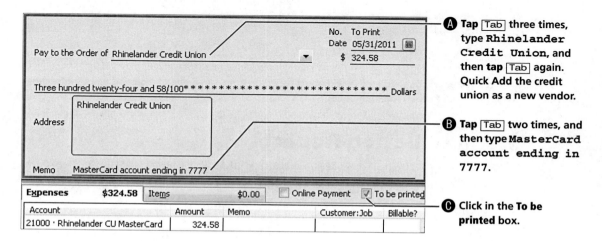

Ⓐ Tap ⌑Tab⌑ three times, type **Rhinelander Credit Union**, and then tap ⌑Tab⌑ again. Quick Add the credit union as a new vendor.

Ⓑ Tap ⌑Tab⌑ two times, and then type **MasterCard account ending in 7777**.

Ⓒ Click in the **To be printed** box.

20. Click Save & Close to record the check and close the window.

21. Close the Chart of Accounts window.

5.6 Working with Banking and Balance Sheet Reports

In this section, you will learn about reports that can tell you stories about your banking activities in QuickBooks as well as those that display information about your balance sheet accounts (asset, liability, and equity). You will also have an opportunity to look at the snapshots available in QuickBooks. In previous versions of QuickBooks, there was just one "snapshot" available to give you general information about your company. In QuickBooks 2011, you can also access snapshots relative to payments and customers.

Banking Reports

The QuickBooks banking feature comes with preset reports for you to use to get answers from your data. Banking reports deal with answers to questions such as:

- What are all of the transactions involving a specific payee?
- What checks have not cleared the bank as of the last bank statement?
- Which payments still need to be deposited?
- Where can I find a list of all transactions that affect my checking account?
- What changes in transactions may affect my next reconciliation?

Register QuickReports

Register QuickReports are run right from a register window. Once you have selected a transaction and clicked the QuickReport button, you will receive a report that shows all transactions for the payee of the selected transaction.

Chez Devereaux Salon and Spa
Register QuickReport

Accrual Basis   All Transactions

Type	Date	Num	Memo	Account	Clr	Split	Amount
Hitchcock Property Management							
Bill Pmt -Check	05/11/2011	3001	LS2009156	10000 · Checking	✓	20000 · Acco...	-500.00
Bill Pmt -Check	05/18/2011	3005	LS2009156	10000 · Checking	✓	20000 · Acco...	-200.00
Total Hitchcock Property Management							-700.00
TOTAL							**-700.00**

This is an example of a register QuickReport based on Chez Devereaux Salon and Spa's transactions with Hitchcock Property Management.

Reconciliation Reports

Reconciliation reports show transactions that have cleared as well as those that have yet to clear the bank. QuickBooks allows you to save reconciliation reports in PDF.

Alternatives to Printing Reports

Of course you can send any report to the printer. QuickBooks also gives you additional options for storing or working with a report:

- **Email:** QuickBooks can convert the report to PDF, which can be viewed with the free Adobe Reader program. This allows viewing of the report exactly as it would print even to those who do not have QuickBooks. In QuickBooks 2011, this feature has been improved. When you choose to email a form or report to a customer, the form or report will automatically be converted to PDF for you.
- **Export:** QuickBooks can export the report to Microsoft Excel so you can use Excel's powerful spreadsheet features to work with your data.

Saving Reports and Forms as PDF

PDF copies of QuickBooks reports and forms make emailing forms and reports convenient for you. They are also a great way to create copies to save for your own records.

 The type of printer driver for PDF printing has been changed for QuickBooks 2011, improving the reliability of this task.

QUICK REFERENCE	PRODUCING BANKING REPORTS
Task	**Procedure**
Produce a register QuickReport	■ Open the register from which you wish to create the report.
	■ Click within the transaction on which you wish to base the report.
	■ Click QuickReport on the register toolbar.
Produce a reconciliation report	■ Choose Reports→Banking→Previous Reconciliation from the menu bar.
	■ Choose the correct account and the statement ending date.
	■ Choose whether you want a detail or summary report (or both), and then click Display.
Produce a reconciliation discrepancy report	■ Choose Reports→Banking→Reconciliation Discrepancy from the menu bar.
	■ Choose the correct account, and then click OK.

DEVELOP YOUR SKILLS 5.6.1

Produce Banking Reports and a PDF Copy of a Report

In this exercise, you will help Bill produce two banking reports and save one of them as a PDF file.

Create a Reconciliation Report

In the last exercise, you reconciled the checking account for Chez Devereaux Salon and Spa. Now you will produce a summary report that documents this task.

1. Choose **Reports→Banking→Previous Reconciliation** from the menu bar.

2. Ensure **10000•Checking** is displayed and that the circle to the left of Detail is selected.

3. Click the **Display** button to produce the report.
QuickBooks generates this report as a PDF file that can be saved, printed, and/or emailed. A copy of this report is displayed at the beginning of this lesson on the case study page.

4. Close the **Reconciliation Detail** report window.

Run a Register QuickReport

You will now create a report based on information contained within your Checking account.

5. Click the **Check Register** task icon in the Banking area of the Home page.

6. Click **OK** to choose the 10000•Checking account.
The Chez Devereaux Salon and Spa Checking register will be displayed.

7. Follow these steps to produce the register QuickReport:

Ⓐ Scroll up until the 5/11/11 transaction for **Hitchcock Property Management** is visible.

Ⓑ Single-click anywhere within the two-line transaction.

Ⓒ Click the **QuickReport** button on the toolbar.

Date	Number	Payee		Payment	✓	Deposit	Balance
	Type	Account	Memo				
04/30/2011	1100	Cranberry Fields Magazine		34.00	✓		20,294.47
	CHK	62500 · Dues and renew magazine su					
05/11/2011	3001	Hitchcock Property Management		500.00	✓		19,794.47
	BILLPMT	20000 · Accounts I LS2009156					
05/11/2011	3002	Brooks Family Insurance		136.54	✓		19,657.93

Toolbar: ⬍ Go to... | 🖨 Print... | ✏ Edit Transaction | 📋 QuickReport | 📄 Download Bank Statement

FROM THE KEYBOARD

Ctrl+q to display a QuickReport

A report will be displayed that shows all of the transactions from the checking register for Hitchcock Property Management. Notice the various buttons on the toolbar that you can use to print, email, export, and perform other tasks with this report. Leave this report open for the next step.

Produce a PDF Copy of a Report

Now you will help Bill save a PDF copy of this report. You will save it in your default file location.

8. Make sure that the QuickReport for **Hitchcock Property Management** is still the active window; then, choose **File→Save as PDF** from the main QuickBooks menu bar.
A Save document as PDF window will appear.

9. Follow these steps to save a copy of the report as a PDF file:

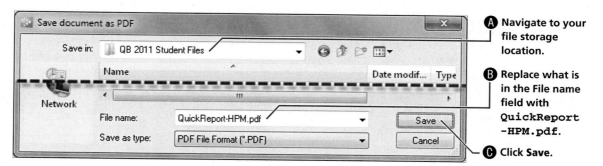

A Navigate to your file storage location.

B Replace what is in the File name field with `QuickReport-HPM.pdf`.

C Click **Save**.

QuickBooks will process the command, saving a copy of the file to your default file location.

10. Choose Window→Close All from the menu bar.

Balance Sheet Reports

In Lesson 4, Working with Customers, you learned how to produce one of the main company reports, Profit & Loss. In this section, you will look at another vital report, the balance sheet report.

Types of Accounts Displayed on a Balance Sheet Report

A balance sheet report displays all of your asset, liability, and equity accounts (hence the designation the "balance sheet accounts"). You can customize your report to show only the accounts you wish to display.

Company Snapshot

The Company Snapshot window gives you a quick view of your company's bottom line in one convenient place. You can customize it to include "at-a-glance" reports that are the most important to your company. The Company Snapshot can be accessed via a button on the icon bar or by choosing Reports→Company Snapshot from the menu bar. The Company Snapshot will show information only within a preset date range. If you don't see anything displayed, it is likely because the date for which you are performing the exercise is past the date range available through the snapshot.

With the 2011 version of QuickBooks, there are two additional snapshots available for use: Customer and Payments.

The Add Content link will open a horizontal scrolling menu from which you can browse for content panels that you wish to include in your Company Snapshot.

The drop-down arrow contained within each panel provides you with options to print, print preview, or save as an image your content panel data.

The Restore Default link will bring back any panels that you have removed, reset any date range changes you made, and remove any panels that you may have added.

Information in the Company Snapshot is contained within content panels, each with its own Close button.

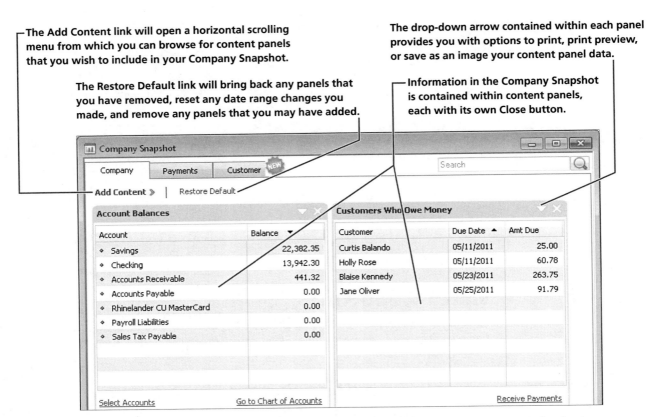

You can customize the Company Snapshot to display information that is of value to you. Notice the three tabs at the top of the window that allow you to switch between the three snapshot views.

QUICK REFERENCE	WORKING WITH BALANCE SHEET REPORTS AND COMPANY SNAPSHOTS
Task	**Procedure**
Produce a balance sheet report	■ Choose Reports→Company & Financial→Balance Sheet Standard from the menu bar.
Produce a Company Snapshot	■ Choose Reports→Company Snapshot from the menu bar. ■ Customize the snapshot to meet your needs.

View a Balance Sheet Report and a Company Snapshot

In this exercise, you will create both a balance sheet report and a company snapshot for Chez Devereaux Salon and Spa.

Create a Balance Sheet Report

When you create a balance sheet report, it will be based as of a certain date rather than for a period of time (as is the case for a profit & loss report).

1. Choose **Reports→Company & Financial→ Balance Sheet Standard** from the menu bar.

2. **Tap** ⃞Tab⃞, type **053111**, and then **tap** ⃞Tab⃞ again.

   QuickBooks displays a balance sheet report showing the asset, liability, and equity account balances as of May 31, 2011.

3. Close the **Balance Sheet** window, choosing not to memorize the report.

Display and Customize the Company Snapshot

You will now help Bill delete a content panel from the company snapshot and then restore the default.

Chez Devereaux Salon and Spa
Balance Sheet

Accrual Basis	As of May 31, 2011	
		⬦ May 31, 11 ⬦
ASSETS		
Current Assets		
Checking/Savings		
10000 · Checking	▶	13,964.80 ◀
10200 · Savings		22,382.35
Total Checking/Savings		36,347.15
Accounts Receivable		
11000 · Accounts Receivable		442.57
Total Accounts Receivable		442.57
Total Current Assets		36,789.72
TOTAL ASSETS		**36,789.72**
LIABILITIES & EQUITY		
Equity		
30000 · Opening Balance Equity		37,815.02
Net Income		-1,025.30
Total Equity		36,789.72
TOTAL LIABILITIES & EQUITY		**36,789.72**

4. Choose **Reports→Company Snapshot** from the menu bar.

   Depending on the actual date that you perform this exercise, you may or may not have information displayed since all of the transactions we have entered up to this point are dated in May 2011. Don't worry about the data displayed in the content panel for this exercise, but rather how to manipulate it.

5. Follow these steps to remove a content panel from the snapshot:

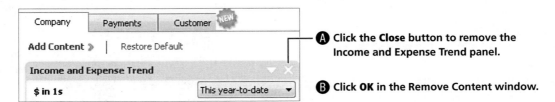

Ⓐ Click the **Close** button to remove the Income and Expense Trend panel.

Ⓑ Click **OK** in the Remove Content window.

Notice that once you have removed the Income and Expense Trend panel, the Account Balances panel "snaps" up into the vacated space. You will now restore the default content panels to the snapshot.

6. Click the **Restore Default** link above the Account Balances panel.

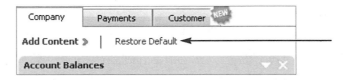

7. Click **OK** in the Restore Default window.

8. Close the **Company Snapshot** window.

9. Once you are finished learning about Banking Online with QuickBooks, choose the appropriate option for your situation:

   ■ If you are continuing on to the next lesson or to the end-of-lesson exercises, leave QuickBooks open and move on to the next exercise.

   ■ If you are finished working in QuickBooks for now, choose **File→Exit** from the menu bar.

5.7 Banking Online with QuickBooks

There are a variety of tasks that can be carried out online with QuickBooks. You can manage your documents, bank online, and pay bills online to name a few. In Lesson 1, Introducing QuickBooks Pro, you learned about QuickBooks Connect, which is an online tool to help you to work with QuickBooks more efficiently.

QuickBooks Attached Documents

With the 2010 version, QuickBooks has made it easier than ever for you to keep track of all business documents in one place. The attached documents feature allows a QuickBooks user to attach electronic documentation (PDF files or scanned documents) to any transaction or to attach documents to a customer, vender, or employee account.

Notice the Attach buttons available in the Vendor Information area of the Vendor Center and on the toolbar of the Enter Credit Card Charges window.

Online Banking Features

QuickBooks contains many online banking features. Some of the program's most useful online banking capabilities enable you to:

- **Access accounts online and download information:** QuickBooks allows you to download transactions and account information once you have set up your account(s) for online banking. You can use this feature to easily reconcile your account, too.
- **Transfer funds online:** If you have more than one account at the same financial institution, you can set up a transfer between accounts in QuickBooks. When you go online with QuickBooks, the transfer will be made for you.
- **Make payments online:** Some financial institutions allow you to pay bills online through QuickBooks. If your institution doesn't offer this service, Intuit has a service to which you can subscribe. To process a check as an online payment, you must set up the vendor by including his name, address, phone number, and account number by which he identifies you in the Vendor List.

Preparing for Online Banking with QuickBooks

Before you can use the online banking features in QuickBooks, you must complete an application with your financial institution and receive a confirmation letter with a personal identification number (PIN) in the mail. Charges for this service vary by financial institution. Contact your financial institution to find out the charges and functionality with QuickBooks.

QUICK REFERENCE	GOING ONLINE WITH QUICKBOOKS
Task	**Procedure**
Learn more about attached documents, including pricing	■ Choose Company→Attached Documents→Learn About Attached Documents from the menu bar. ■ Click the "subscribe here" link to launch a webpage with more information.
Set up an account for online access	■ Contact your financial institution and complete an application for QuickBooks online services. ■ Choose Banking→Online Banking→Setup Account for Online Services once you have received the PIN from your financial institution. ■ Progress through the steps in the Setup Account for Online Services interview.

5.8 Concepts Review

Concepts Review   labyrinthelab.com/qb11_level01

To test your knowledge of the key concepts introduced in this lesson, complete the Concepts Review quiz by going to the URL listed above.

Reinforce Your Skills

Before you begin the Reinforce Your Skills exercises, complete one of these options:

- Open the file *[Your name]'s Tea Shoppe at the Lake* from your file storage location that you used for Lesson 4.

- Restore the *Lesson 5 Tea Shoppe at the Lake* file from your file storage location. If you need to review how to restore a portable company file, take a peek at Develop Your Skills 3.1.1. Make sure to place your name as the first word in the company filename (e.g., *Susie's Tea Shoppe at the Lake*).

REINFORCE YOUR SKILLS 5.1
Work with Bank Accounts and Make a Deposit

In this exercise, you will take care of the banking tasks for The Tea Shoppe.

Create a Money Market Account

Susie's business checking account earns no interest so she has decided to open a money market account at the same bank.

1. Choose **Lists→Chart of Accounts** from the menu bar.

2. Click the **Account** menu button and choose **New**.

3. Choose **Bank** as the account type, and then click **Continue**.

4. Type **Money Market** as the new account name.

5. Click **Save & Close**, choosing **No** in the Set Up Online Services window.

6. Close the **Chart of Accounts** window.

Transfer Funds between Accounts

Since the money market account earns interest, Susie has decided to transfer some funds from her checking account into it.

7. Choose **Banking→Transfer Funds** from the menu bar.

8. Set the date to **6/1/11**.

9. Choose **Checking** as the Transfer Funds From account.

10. Choose **Money Market** as the Transfer Funds To account.

11. Type **10000** as the transfer amount.

12. Click **Save & Close** to record the transfer and close the window.

Make Deposits

Susie did a cooking demonstration for a local organization. She needs to deposit the fee she earned into her checking account along with the funds that are currently in the Undeposited Funds account. You will do this in two separate steps

13. Choose **Banking→Make Deposits** from the menu bar.

14. Select all five of the payments in the **Payments to Deposit** window, and then click **OK**.

15. Ensure **Checking** is the Deposit To account. Click **OK** if the default account information window appears in order to acknowledge it and move to the Make Deposits window.

16. Set the deposit date as **6/25/11**, and then click **Save & New**.

17. Change the Date for the next deposit to **6/27/11**, **tap** Tab, and then type **cooking demonstration** as the memo.

18. Click in the **From Account** column, and then type **cat** to fill in Catering Sales as the income account.
    Remember, you do not have to enter a customer, but you must enter an income account!

19. Enter the payment in the form of a check: number **753** for **$800**.
    Your screen should resemble the following illustration.

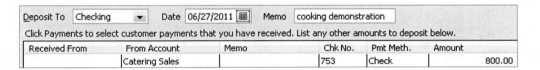

20. Click **Save & Close** to record the transaction and close the window.

Reconcile a Bank Account

The bank statement has just arrived, so it is time to reconcile it to the Tea Shoppe's QuickBooks account. You may print your own statement (Reinforce Your Skills 5.2 Bank Statement) from your default storage location or refer to the illustration shown after step 2.

Reconcile the Checking Account

1. Choose **Banking→Reconcile** from the menu bar.

2. Using the statement you printed or the following copy, reconcile the Checking account for Susie.

ROP Credit Union
9235 Kirkland Way
Lake San Marcos, CA 92078

Statement of Account Prepared For:
The Tea Shoppe at the Lake
Susie Elsasser
316 Swan Drive
Lake San Marcos, CA 92078

Account Number: 555-777

Statement Period: May 1 - May 31, 2011

Total Deposits:	$9,878.00	Total Payments:	$5,682.35
Beginning Balance:	$13,953.99	Ending Balance:	$18,149.64

Transactions:

Date	Transaction type	Payment	Deposit	Balance
	Beginning Balance			$13,953.99
5/6/2011	Check #1102	1,000.00		$12,953.99
5/7/2011	Deposit		2,510.00	15,463.99
5/7/2011	Check #1081	55.73		15,408.26
5/7/2011	Check #1082	779.00		14,629.26
5/7/2011	Check #1083	163.00		14,466.26
5/7/2011	Check #1084	186.00		14,280.26
5/7/2011	Check #1085	124.00		14,156.26
5/7/2011	Check #1086	202.63		13,953.63
5/14/2011	Deposit		2,463.00	16,416.63
5/14/2011	Check #1087	175.00		16,241.63
5/14/2011	Check #1088	175.00		16,066.63
5/14/2011	Check #1089	130.00		15,936.63
5/14/2011	Check #1090	84.99		15,851.64
5/20/2011	Check #1103	1,000.00		14,851.64
5/20/2011	Check #1104	125.00		14,726.64
5/21/2011	Deposit		2,500.00	17,226.64
5/21/2011	Check #1105	782.00		16,444.64
5/21/2011	Check #1106	349.00		16,095.64
5/21/2011	Check #1107	170.00		15,925.64
5/21/2011	Check #1108	171.00		15,754.64
5/28/2011	Deposit		2,405.00	18,159.64
5/31/2011	Service Charge	10.00		18,149.64
	Ending Balance			18,149.64

Pay attention to the following hints when you reconcile:

- *In the Begin Reconciliation window, make sure to enter the ending balance and the service charge.*

- *In the Reconcile-Checking window, make sure to mark only those transactions that have cleared the bank (and are on the bank statement) and that have zero differences before you click Reconcile Now.*

- *If the difference is not zero, see the Problem Resolution Process section on page 172.*

3. Choose to not create a reconciliation report now.

Manage Credit Card Transactions

In this exercise, you will help Susie set up her new Visa credit card in QuickBooks.

Create a New Credit Card Account

1. If your Chart of Accounts window is not open, choose **Lists→Chart of Accounts** from the menu bar.

2. Click the **Account** menu button and choose **New** from the context menu.

3. Choose **Credit Card** as the account type, and then click **Continue**.

4. Name the new account **ROP CU Visa**.

5. Click **Save & Close** to enter the new account and close the window, choosing **No** when asked if you want to set up online services.

Enter a Credit Card Charge

Susie is purchasing new aprons for the business. She is not sure of the color for one of the aprons, so she will purchase two and later return one of them.

6. Choose **Banking→Enter Credit Card Charges** from the menu bar.

7. **Tap** Tab three times and type **Betty's Boutique** as the vendor. **Tap** Tab again, and then choose to **Quick Add** the boutique as a vendor.

8. Set the date to **6/2/11**, **tap** Tab twice, and then type **$150** as the amount.

9. Click in the **Account** column and choose **Uniforms & Linens** as the expense account.

10. Click **Save & New** to record the transaction.

Enter a Credit Card Credit

Now you will process the uniform return for Susie. The Enter Credit Card Charges window should still be open from the last step; if it isn't, choose Banking→Record Credit Card Charges→Enter Credit Card Charges from the menu bar.

11. Choose **Betty's Boutique** as the vendor.

12. Set the date to **6/6/11**.

13. Choose the **Refund/Credit** option to show it is a return.

14. Type **$30** as the amount and ensure that Uniforms & Linens is the account.

15. Click **Save & Close** to record the refund and close the window.

Produce Banking and Balance Sheet Reports

Susie wants to run some banking reports to get answers from her data. In this exercise, you will help her do just that.

Produce a Reconciliation Report

Susie already performed a reconciliation; now you will produce the reconciliation report for her.

1. Choose **Reports→Banking→Previous Reconciliation** from the menu bar.

2. Choose to create a **Summary** report for the reconciliation you just performed (statement ending date of 5/31/2011).

3. Click **Display** to produce the report.

4. Preview how the report will print, and then close the **Reconciliation Summary** window.

Run a Deposit Detail Report

Susie would like to see all of her bank deposits for June, so she will run a report to display them.

5. Choose **Reports→Banking→Deposit Detail** from the menu bar.

6. Tap ⟨Tab⟩, and type **060111**; tap ⟨Tab⟩ again and type **063011**.

7. Click the Refresh button on the report toolbar.
   You will see a report that displays the details for each deposit in May.

 If you tap ⟨Tab⟩ after changing the date, QuickBooks will automatically refresh the report for you, too.

8. Choose **File→Save as PDF** from the menu bar.

9. Choose to save a copy of the report in your default storage location, naming it **June 2011 Deposits**.

10. Close the **Deposit Details** report window, clicking **No** when asked to memorize the report.

Display a Balance Sheet Report

11. Choose **Reports→Company & Financial→Balance Sheet Standard** from the menu bar.

12. Tap ⟨a⟩ to change the date range to All.

13. Choose **Window→Close All** from the menu bar.

14. Choose the appropriate option for your situation:
    - If you are continuing on to the rest of the end-of-lesson exercises, leave QuickBooks open.
    - If you are finished working in QuickBooks for now, choose **File→Exit** from the menu bar.

Apply Your Skills

Before you begin these exercises, restore the Wet Noses Veterinary Clinic Lesson 5 (Portable) file or open the file that you used for the Apply Your Skills exercise in Lesson 4. Name the file **[Your Name]'s Wet Noses Vet Clinic**. *If you need to review how to restore a portable company file, follow steps 1–8 in Develop Your Skills 3.1.1.*

Manage Banking and Deposits

In this exercise, you will help Dr. James with some basic banking tasks.

1. Open the **Chart of Accounts** and create two new accounts for Wet Noses: a bank account named Money Market and a credit card account named American Express. Choose to not set up online services for either account.

2. Open the **Make Deposits** window and choose to deposit all four payments from the Undeposited Funds account into your Checking account on 6/8/11.

3. Open the **Transfer Funds** window and transfer $30,000 from Checking to Money Market on 6/10/11.

Enter Credit Card Transactions

You will now enter transactions into the credit card account you just created.

1. Choose **Banking→Enter Credit Card Charges** from the menu bar.

2. Enter the following American Express charges for the month.
   Quick Add any vendors not on the Vendor List and use your best judgment in selecting an expense account.

Date	Vendor	Amount	Memo
6/1/11	Thrifty Grocery	$26.73	Bottled water and soda for office
6/4/11	Glen's Handyman Service	$108.70	Office repairs
6/4/11	Malimali Hardware Store	$43.20	Supplies for office repairs
6/8/11	Labyrinth Veterinary Publications	$94.85	Reference books
6/11/11	Thrifty Grocery	$18.49	Refreshments for office
6/14/11	Bothell Pet Supply Co.	$115.43	Boarding supplies
6/14/11	Murray Gardening Service	$60.00	Monthly garden maintenance
6/20/11	Beezer Computer Repair	$145.00	Computer repair
6/20/11	Bothell Pet Supply Co.	-$38.29	Return-Boarding supplies
6/22/11	Laura's Café	30.21	Business lunch with partner

3. Close the **Enter Credit Card Charges** window when you are finished.

Reconcile a Credit Card Account

In this exercise, you will reconcile the American Express account.

1. Open the **Chart of Accounts** and begin the process to reconcile the American Express account using the following illustration.

```
┌─────────────────────────────────────────────────────────────┐
│                     American Express                          │
│                      6539 Beck Place                          │
│                     New York, NY 07852                        │
│                                                               │
│ Credit Card Statement Prepared For:                           │
│   Wet Noses Veterinary Clinic                                 │
│   589 Retriever Drive                                         │
│   Bothell, WA 98011                                           │
│                          Account Number: 3333-888888-55555    │
│                                                               │
│                          Statement Period: May 21 - June 20, 2011 │
├─────────────────────────────┬───────────────────────────────┤
│   Total                     │        Total                  │
│   Charges:    612.40        │        Credits:    $38.29     │
│   Beginning                 │        Ending                 │
│   Balance:    $0.00         │        Balance:    $574.11    │
├─────────────────────────────┴───────────────────────────────┤
│ Transactions:                                                 │
│   Date        Description        Charge   Credit   Balance    │
│               Beginning Balance                     $0.00     │
│   6/1/2011    Thrifty Grocery     26.73            $26.73     │
│   6/4/2011    Glen's Handyman    108.70            $135.43    │
│   6/4/2011    Malimali Hardware Store 43.20        $178.63    │
│   6/8/2011    Laby Vet Pub        94.85            $273.48    │
│   6/11/2011   Thrifty Grocery     18.49            $291.97    │
│   6/14/2011   Bothell Pet Supply 115.43            $407.40    │
│   6/14/2011   Murray Gardening Service 60.00       $467.40    │
│   6/20/2011   Beezer Computer    145.00            $612.40    │
│   6/20/2011   Bothell Pet Supply           38.29   $574.11    │
│               Periodic Finance Charge   0          $574.11    │
│               Ending Balance                       $574.11    │
└───────────────────────────────────────────────────────────────┘
```

2. When you have completed the reconciliation, write a check to American Express for the entire amount, choosing for it to be printed. Then, print a summary reconciliation report.

Answer Questions with Reports

In this exercise, you will answer questions for Dr. James by running reports. You may wish to display the Report Center in List View to help you answer the questions. Ask your instructor if you should print the reports or simply display them on the screen.

1. What are the details of the checks that have been written?

2. What transactions were not cleared when the American Express account was reconciled?

3. Is it possible to get a detailed list of all deposits for May?

4. Are there any missing or duplicate check numbers?

5. What is the balance of all of the balance sheet accounts as of June 22, 2011?

6. Choose the appropriate option for your situation:

   ■ If you are continuing on to the Critical Thinking exercises, leave QuickBooks open.

   ■ If you are finished working in QuickBooks for now, choose **File→Exit** from the menu bar.

Critical Thinking

In the course of working through the following Critical Thinking exercises, you will be utilizing various skills taught in this and previous lesson(s). Take your time and think carefully about the tasks presented to you. Turn back to the lesson content if you need assistance.

5.1 Sort Through the Stack

Before You Begin: Restore the Monkey Business Lesson 5 (Portable) file from your storage location. (Remember that the password is blank for Mary!)

You have been hired by Mary Minard to help her with her organization's books. She is the owner of Monkey Business, a nonprofit organization that provides low-income students with help in preparing for college placement exams and applying for scholarships. You have just sat down at her desk and found a pile of papers. It is your job to sort through the papers and make sense of what you find, entering information into QuickBooks whenever appropriate, and answering any other questions in a word processing document saved as **Critical Thinking 5-1**.

- Scribbled on a scrap of paper: I looked at QuickBooks and saw money in an account called "Undeposited Funds." Why isn't it in the Checking account? Can you move it for me? I deposited those funds into the Checking account on 7/11/2011!

- New credit card document on desk: From Jasper State Credit Union, number 7777 2222 0000 2938, $7,500 credit limit.

- Note: Opened a new Money Market bank account at Jasper State Credit Union on 7/10/11. Transferred $10,000 from Savings to fund the new account. Need QuickBooks account set up.

- Bank deposit slip: Check #2323 dated 7/14/2011 for a $2,500 deposit to Checking. Hand-written message on slip reads, "From Hanson Family Trust."

- Credit card receipt: Dated 7/15/2011; for cups, cookies, and napkins; $24.11; paid to Cherry City Supermart.

- Note: Would you please create a report that shows all of the activity in the Checking account for July 2011 and save it as a PDF file so I can email it to the accountant?

- Bank deposit slip: Dated 7/30/2011 for $500; handwritten on slip, check #3889 from Lakeside Christian School for payment toward invoice for College 101 seminar on 7/27/2011.

- Credit card receipt: Dated 7/23/2011; payable to Casey's Service Station; for auto fuel; amount of $35.61. (Hint: This is for travel to a school site.)

- Scribbled note from Mary: Can you produce a report for me that shows the balances for all of the asset, liability, and equity accounts as of 7/31/2011?

5.2 Tackle the Tasks

Now is your chance to work a little more with Chez Devereaux Salon and Spa and apply the skills that you have learned in this lesson to accomplish additional tasks. Restore the Critical Thinking 5.2 portable company file from your file storage location. Then, enter the following tasks.

Create banking accounts	Use the following information to create two new accounts: 10400•Money Market; Rhinelander Credit Union 22000•American Express
Make a deposit	On 6/1/11, provide a haircut and manicure to Holly Rose for cash (use a Sales Receipt). Deposit the funds from Undeposited Funds to Checking on the same day.
Transfer funds	On 6/3/11, transfer $1,000 from Checking to Money Market.
Enter credit card transactions	Enter the following American Express transactions: On 6/2/11, purchase a customer appreciation lunch from Home Place Pizzaria (add as a new vendor) for $65.11, using the 64300•Meals and Entertainment account. On 6/4/11, purchase bottled water and cookies from Cost Club for $25.67, using 61500•Client Refreshments as the account.
Produce reports	Display a summary previous reconciliation report for the Checking account. Display a balance sheet detail report as of 6/4/11.

Need to Know Accounting

IN THIS APPENDIX

Even though QuickBooks does everything for you "behind the scenes," it is important that you have a basic understanding of what is happening to your books.

In this appendix, you will learn about the basic financial statements important to any business and the accounts that appear on these reports. You will also learn about the double-entry accounting system and the debits and credits that must always be equal.

There are two main reports that a company will produce periodically to illustrate its financial well-being.

■ A **Balance Sheet** report displays all of the holdings of the company along with the debts as of a particular date.

■ An **Income Statement**, otherwise known as a Profit & Loss Report, displays the income and expenses for a specified period of time.

Understanding the accounts that make up each of these reports is key to understanding your company's books.

The Accounting Equation and the Balance Sheet

The first equation you need to learn when it comes to accounting is simply termed the accounting equation:

$$\text{Assets} = \text{Liabilities} + \text{Equity}$$

This means that if you take all of your company's debt and add any investments (equity), you will have a value equal to all of the assets that your company owns.

A balance sheet is a financial statement that displays all asset, liability, and equity accounts (the balance sheet accounts). Take a look at the following illustrations to see how the accounting equation works and is represented in a balance sheet:

The upper section of the balance sheet represents the left side of the accounting equation and displays all of the assets.

The Tea Shoppe at the Lake
Balance Sheet
As of July 31, 2011

	◇ Jul 31, 11 ◇
ASSETS	
Current Assets	
Checking/Savings	
Checking	▶ 22,964.90 ◀
Money Market	10,000.00
Petty Cash	178.13
Total Checking/Savings	33,143.03
Accounts Receivable	
Accounts Receivable	1,833.49
Total Accounts Receivable	1,833.49
Other Current Assets	
Inventory Asset	280.00
Prepaid Rent	4,600.00
Total Other Current Assets	4,880.00
Total Current Assets	39,856.52
Fixed Assets	
Accumulated Depreciation	-560.00
Furniture and Equipment	11,689.00
Total Fixed Assets	11,129.00
TOTAL ASSETS	**50,985.52**

Notice that the amount for Total Assets is $50,985.52

The lower section of the balance sheet represents the right side of the accounting equation and displays all of the liability and equity accounts.

The Tea Shoppe at the Lake
Balance Sheet
As of July 31, 2011

	◇ Jul 31, 11 ◇
LIABILITIES & EQUITY	
Liabilities	
Current Liabilities	
Accounts Payable	
Accounts Payable	1,526.04
Total Accounts Payable	1,526.04
Credit Cards	
American Express	578.51
ROP CU Visa	120.00
Total Credit Cards	698.51
Other Current Liabilities	
Sales Tax Payable	257.06
Total Other Current Liabilities	257.06
Total Current Liabilities	2,481.61
Long Term Liabilities	
Steamer Loan	2,000.00
Total Long Term Liabilities	2,000.00
Total Liabilities	4,481.61
Equity	
Owner's Equity	19,120.00
Owner Draw	-8,000.00
Net Income	35,383.91
Total Equity	46,503.91
TOTAL LIABILITIES & EQUITY	**50,985.52**

Notice that the amount for Total Liabilities & Equity is also $50,985.52.

The Income Statement

The accounts that you find on the Income Statement (or Profit & Loss report) are income and expense. In the following illustration you can view an Income Statement and the accounts that appear on it.

The Tea Shoppe at the Lake
Profit & Loss
May through July 2011

	◇ May - Jul 11 ◇
Ordinary Income/Expense	
Income	
Beverage Sales	▶ 19,347.00 ◀
Catering Sales	4,215.75
Craft Sales	450.00
Food Sales	10,208.00
Total Income	34,220.75
Cost of Goods Sold	
Cost of Goods Sold	210.00
Food Purchases	2,115.87
Restaurant Supplies	999.97
Total COGS	3,325.84
Gross Profit	30,894.91
Expense	
Advertising and Promotion	733.00
Bank Service Charges	10.00
Business Licenses and Permits	125.00
Depreciation Expense	560.00
Insurance Expense	389.00
Office Supplies	170.13
Rent Expense	2,300.00
Uniforms & Linens	120.00
Utilities	471.04
Vendor Credits	-106.94
Total Expense	4,771.23
Net Ordinary Income	26,123.68
Net Income	26,123.68

The total of all your income accounts will result in your Gross Profit.

The Total Expense is totaled below the Gross Profit.

The difference between the Gross Profit and Total Expense results in the Net Income (or Net Loss if the expenses are greater than the income).

A.2 Debits and Credits: The Double-Entry Accounting System

There is another equation in accounting that is paramount for us to keep in mind: Debits must always equal credits! Most people who do not work in the accounting field are confused about debits and credits, though.

Accounts are often displayed in a "T" format in accounting (which you can see in all of the Behind the Scenes sections of this book). The T accounts allow you to place the name of the account on the top, account debits on the left side, and account credits on the right side. This means that the left side (debits) must always equal the right side (credits) when entering accounting transactions (hence the term "double-entry").

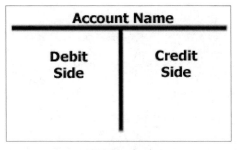

A simple way to view an account is to use the T format.

In order to understand debits and credits a bit better, we will now look at the types of accounts and their normal balances.

Types of Accounts and Normal Balances

We have looked at the two main financial statements and the types of accounts included in each. The balance sheet is composed of asset, liability, and equity accounts. The income statement is composed of income and expense accounts. Before we look deeper into each account type, it is important to understand normal balances.

Take a look at Lesson 2, Creating a Company, to view all of the account sub-types that you can create in QuickBooks.

About Normal Balances

Each type of account must have a normal balance of either a debit or a credit. The normal balance is the side that will increase the amount of the account. Assets and expenses both have debit normal balances and will increase when debited and decrease when credited. Liabilities, equity, and income all have credit normal balances and will increase when credited and decrease when debited.

The concept of normal balances makes sense if you think of the balance sheet. Assets with a debit normal balance must equal the sum of the liabilities and equity, which both have a credit normal balance. Think of this as the marriage of the accounting equation and the fact that debits must equal credits!

The following table describes the primary account types and their normal balances.

Account Type	Description
Assets	An asset is anything that a company owns or monies that are owed to the company. Examples of assets are checking accounts, accounts receivable, and autos. Assets have a debit normal balance.
Liabilities	A liability is something that a company owes such as an auto loan or a credit card balance. Liabilities have a credit normal balance.
Equity	Equity accounts are both investments into the company (Owner's Equity or Stockholder's Equity) and the net income or loss from the operation of a business (Retained Earnings). Equity accounts have a credit normal balance.
Income	Income accounts reflect the sales and fees earned during an accounting period. Income accounts have a credit normal balance.
Expenses	Expense accounts record the expenditures that a company accrues while conducting business. Expense accounts have a debit normal balance.

The Trial Balance Report

At the end of an accounting cycle a trial balance is prepared that shows all accounts affected during the cycle. The balance of each account is entered in the appropriate column based on its normal balance. The net income or net loss is the difference between income and expenses. If the income is greater than the expenses, an excess credit balance will result and will increase the equity account (a net income). If the expenses are greater than the income, an excess debit balance will result and will decrease the equity account (a net loss).

Look at the following illustration of a trial balance to see how everything we have discussed is pulled together. The difference between the total income ($53,013.94) and the total expenses ($27,424.27) results in a net income of $25,589.67 that will credit (increase) the equity account when the books are closed.

The Tea Shoppe at the Lake
Trial Balance
As of June 30, 2011

	Jun 30, 11	
	Debit	Credit
Checking	12,411.58	
Money Market	10,000.00	
Accounts Receivable	0.00	
Prepaid Rent	5,750.00	
Undeposited Funds	0.00	
Furniture and Equipment	9,120.00	
Accounts Payable		451.91
American Express	0.00	
ROP CU Visa		120.00
Sales Tax Payable	0.00	
Owner's Equity		19,120.00
Owner Draw	8,000.00	
Beverage Sales		33,351.00
Catering Sales		1,550.00
Food Sales		18,006.00
Food Purchases	13,249.00	
Restaurant Supplies	1,960.07	
Advertising and Promotion	1,396.00	
Bank Service Charges	40.00	
Business Licenses and Permits	125.00	
Computer and Internet Expenses	232.86	
Insurance Expense	1,556.00	
Office Supplies	407.25	
Professional Fees	575.00	
Rent Expense	5,950.00	
Repairs and Maintenance	247.00	
Uniforms & Linens	374.97	
Utilities	1,311.12	
Vendor Credits		106.94
TOTAL	**72,705.85**	**72,705.85**

The debits and credits in a Trial Balance must be equal.

A.3 Finding Additional Accounting Resources

Want to learn more about what happens to your company's books behind the scenes in Quick-Books? Visit the website for this course at labyrinthelab.com/qb11_level01 to explore a variety of online learning resources or purchase a copy of *The ABCs of Accounting*, which is also published by Labyrinth Learning.

Glossary

Accrual Basis
In the accrual basis of accounting, income is recorded when the sale is made and expenses recorded when accrued; often used by firms or businesses with large inventories

Activities
Affect what is happening behind the scenes; can be easily input into forms such as invoices or bills

Administrator
QuickBooks user who controls the access of all users of a QuickBooks file; administrator also controls all company preferences in the Edit Preferences window

Assets
Anything owned by a company or that is owed to a company; items such as a checking account, a building, a prepaid insurance account, or accounts receivable

Attached Documents
Feature that allows you to store your source documents electronically, attaching them to the transactions or list entries to which they belong

Backup
The process of creating a condensed copy of your QuickBooks file to ensure you don't lose your data or to allow yourself or another person the ability to view your company file on another computer

Behind the Scenes
The accounting that QuickBooks performs for you when you enter transactions

Browser
A software application used to locate and display web pages, such as Netscape Navigator and Microsoft Internet Explorer

Cash Basis
In the cash basis of accounting, income is recorded when cash is received and expenses recorded when cash is paid; commonly used by small businesses and professionals

Centers
QuickBooks has four centers: Customer, Employee, Report, and Vendor; centers allow you to view the Customers & Jobs, Employee, and Vendor lists, access QuickBooks reports, and view snapshots of information (of an individual customer, vendor, or employee)

Classes
Classes are used to rate; not tied to any particular customer, vendor, or item; used to track only one particular aspect of your business, such as location or individual programs

Closing the Books
During this process at the end of your fiscal year, QuickBooks transfers the net income or net loss to Retained Earnings, restricts access to transactions prior to the closing date (unless you know the password) and allows you to clean up your company data; you are not required to "close the books" in QuickBooks

Company Setup
Takes you through the steps necessary to set up a new company in QuickBooks

Customers & Jobs List
A list in QuickBooks that stores all information related to your customers and the jobs associated with them

Draw
An owner's withdrawal of funds from the company

EasyStep Interview
This method of company creation takes you through a series of questions; your answer to each question determines how your company is set up

Edition
Intuit creates a multitude of editions of QuickBooks to choose from: QuickBooks Basic, QuickBooks Pro, and QuickBooks Premier

Field
A box into which data is entered

File Storage Location
Location in which you store file for this course (USB flash drive, the My Documents folder, or to a network drive at a school or company)

Fonts
QuickBooks displays its preset reports in a default font; you can make many changes as to the characteristics of the font in your report, such as the font name, style, color, and size

Formatting
Formatting deals with the appearance of the report; it has nothing to do with the data contained within it

Generally Accepted Accounting Principles (GAAP)
Rules used to prepare, present, and report financial statements for a wide variety of entities

Graphs
Graphs in QuickBooks allow you to display your information in a more illustrative way

Header and Footer
Default headers and footers appear on all preset QuickBooks reports; change the information included along with how it is formatted on the Header and Footer tabs of the Additional Customization window

Homepage
A web page that serves as an index or table of contents to other documents stored on the site; the main page for a large website; the web page that comes up by default when you open your browser

Hypertext Markup Language (HTML)
A text-based language that any computer can read; used to organize pages with devices such as headings, paragraphs, lists, etc.

Internet
A collection of computers all over the world that send, receive, and store information; access is gained through an Internet Service Provider (ISP); the web is just a portion of the Internet

Investment
Occurs when an owner deposits funds into the company

Just in Time Transaction History
Allows you to see summary information when entering a transaction for a customer or vendor

Link
Also called hyperlink; provides navigation through a website; displayed on the QuickBooks Home page to provide navigation throughout the QuickBooks program

List (Database)
Allows you to store information about customers, vendors, employees, and other data important to your business

Live Community
A place where a user can collaborate with other QuickBooks users to get advice or to provide insights

Long Term Liabilities Account
A QuickBooks account that tracks a liability (loan) you do not plan to pay off within the next year

Online Backup
QuickBooks offers an online backup option for a monthly fee that is determined based on the amount of room you wish to have available for your backup work

On the Fly
When you type a new entry into a field that draws from a list, QuickBooks gives you the opportunity to add the record to the list "on the fly" as you create the transaction

Passing an Expense On to Customers
The process of identifying an expense in a transaction for which you plan to charge a customer and invoicing the customer for the expense

Preferences
The way you interact with QuickBooks is controlled by the preferences you select; the Preferences window has 19 categories; company preferences are controlled by the administrator and determine how the entire company interacts with QuickBooks; personal preferences are controlled by individual users and dictate interactions between QuickBooks and only that one user

Price Level List
Allows a user to set and charge different price levels for different customers or jobs

QuickBooks Connect
Allows users to access their QuickBooks data online or on their mobile phones

Quick Reference Tables
Tables that summarize the tasks you have just learned. Use them as guidelines when you begin work on your own Quick-Books company file.

Quick Report
A report that shows all the transactions recorded in QuickBooks for a particular list record, which can be run from the various list windows

QuickZoom
A QuickBooks report and graph feature that allows you to zoom through underlying sub-reports until you reach the form where the data were originally entered; this can be extremely useful if you have questions about where a figure in a report or graph comes from

Reconciliation
The process of matching your QuickBooks accounts to the bank and credit card statements you receive. It is important to make sure that your account records in QuickBooks match those of the bank or credit card company

Report
A way to display your company information in various ways such as printed, onscreen, or as a PDF file

Resize
To change the height or width of an image, window, or object

Restoring
The process of decompressing a QuickBooks backup or portable company file; when you restore a file in the same location with the same name as another file, it will replace that file

Skip Interview
In this method of company creation, QuickBooks asks you for your basic company information, and it will be up to you to set up certain items such as payroll and inventory later

Starter Chart of Accounts
During the setup process, QuickBooks asks you to choose the business type that your company most closely resembles; QuickBooks uses your choice to create a Chart of Accounts close to what you need (it will take you less time to edit it to fit your unique business than to start from scratch); you cannot change the business type option later

Statement of Cash Flows
Report that shows how viable a company is in the short term; demonstrates whether a company will be able to pay its bills, payroll, and other expenses; also indicates the financial health of the company

Subaccounts
Help you keep precise records; to track expenses more closely, you may want to have separate accounts for your office phone, office fax, cellular phone, etc.; subaccounts are a great way to track these separate expenses while keeping the number of expense accounts down

Template
A specific form format (with no data) on which you can base all of your future forms; QuickBooks provides several templates, but you can also create custom templates

Uniform Resource Locator (URL)
A web address used to identify a unique page on the Internet

Units of Measure
Feature that allows you to convert units of measure; useful for companies that purchase and sell in different units of measure or need to indicate units on purchase or sales forms; available in the Premier and higher versions of QuickBooks

Users
You can set up an unlimited number of users for your QuickBooks company and assign a password for each person; users can only change their own personal preferences (the administrator controls the access each user has to the QuickBooks file)

Vendor
Anyone (except employees) to whom you pay money; could be the electric company, the organization to which you pay taxes, a merchandise supplier, or subcontractors you pay to do work for your customers

Vendor List
A list in QuickBooks that stores all information related to your vendors

Version
Intuit creates a new version of QuickBooks each year (such as QuickBooks 2006, 2007, or 2008) and each new version provides additional features that are new for that year

Website
Refers to a collection of related web pages and their supporting files and folders.

World Wide Web (WWW)
Also called the web; organized system of Internet servers that support HTML documents; the fun part of the Internet

Index

Notes

Notes

Notes

Notes

Notes

Notes

Notes

Instructor: Don

PBA @ verizon.net

214-681-5382

We're working w/ QB accountant

"Contal M" for memorizing invoicing of tenants.